Max Axiom
AND THE SOCIETY OF SUPER SCIENTISTS

FOOD SCARCITY AND HUNGER

BY MYRA FAYE TURNER

ILLUSTRATED BY KATHARINE DOESCHER

CAPSTONE PRESS
a capstone imprint

Published by Capstone Press, an imprint of Capstone.
1710 Roe Crest Drive
North Mankato, Minnesota 56003
capstonepub.com

Library of Congress Cataloging-in-Publication Data
Names: Turner, Myra Faye, author. | Doescher, Katharine, illustrator.
Title: Food scarcity and hunger : a Max Axiom super scientist adventure /
  by Myra Faye Turner ; illustrated by Katharine Doescher.
Description: North Mankato, Minnesota : Capstone Press, [2022] |
  Series: Max Axiom and the Society of Super Scientists | Includes
  bibliographical references and index. | Audience: Ages 8-11 | Audience:
  Grades 4-6
Summary: "Every year, the world's farmers produce a lot of food for
  people to eat. Yet every night, millions of people around the world go
  to bed hungry. Why are people going without food when the earth is able
  to produce so much? In this nonfiction graphic novel, Max Axiom and
  the Society of Super Scientists go on a fact-finding mission to discover the
  reasons behind food scarcity. Young readers can join the team to find
  out why many people deal with food insecurity and learn ways that they
  can help"-- Provided by publisher.
Identifiers: LCCN 2021029910 (print) | LCCN 2021029911 (ebook) |
  ISBN 9781663959188 (hardcover) | ISBN 9781666322606 (paperback) |
  ISBN 9781666322613 (pdf) | ISBN 9781666322637 (kindle edition)
Subjects: LCSH: Food supply--Juvenile literature. | Food security--Juvenile
  literature. | Hunger--Juvenile literature. | Graphic novels.
Classification: LCC HD9000.5 .T836 2022 (print) | LCC HD9000.5 (ebook) |
  DDC 338.1/9--dc23
LC record available at https://lccn.loc.gov/2021029910
LC ebook record available at https://lccn.loc.gov/2021029911

Editorial Credits
Editor: Aaron Sautter; Designer: Brann Garvey; Media Researcher: Morgan
Walters; Production Specialist: Laura Manthe

All internet sites appearing in back matter were available and accurate
when this book was sent to press.

TABLE OF CONTENTS

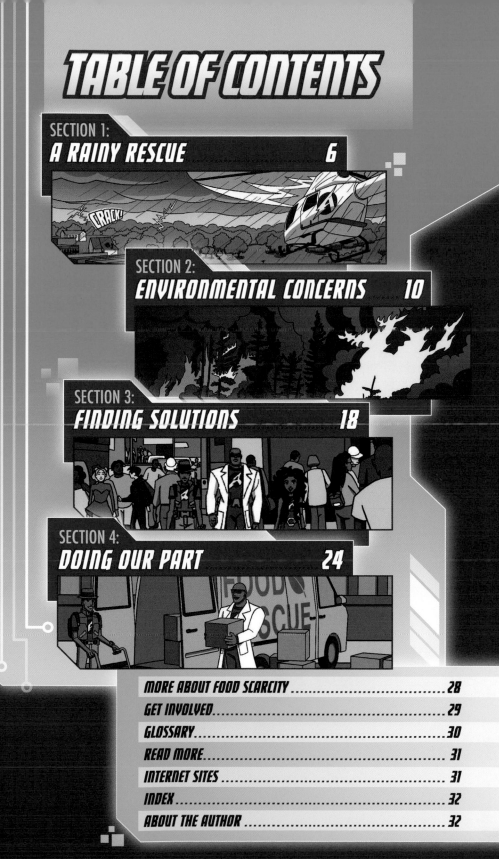

THE SOCIETY OF SUPER SCIENTISTS

MAX AXIOM

After years of study, Max Axiom, the world's first Super Scientist, knew the mysteries of the universe were too vast for one person alone to uncover. So Max created the Society of Super Scientists! Using their superpowers and super-smarts, this talented group investigates today's most urgent scientific and environmental issues and learns about actions everyone can take to solve them.

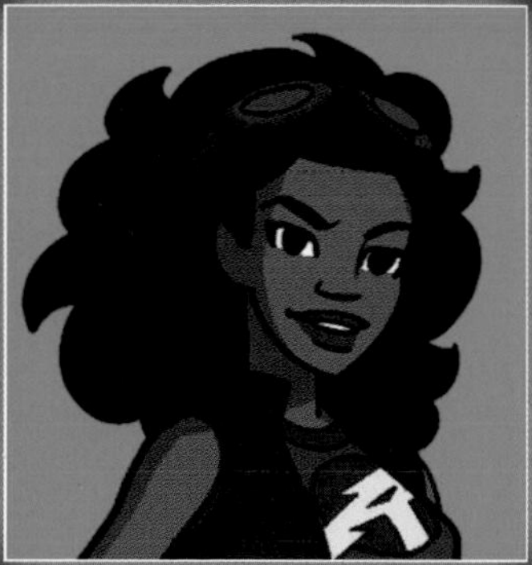

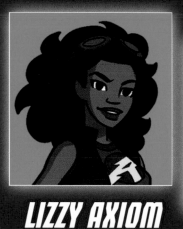

LIZZY AXIOM

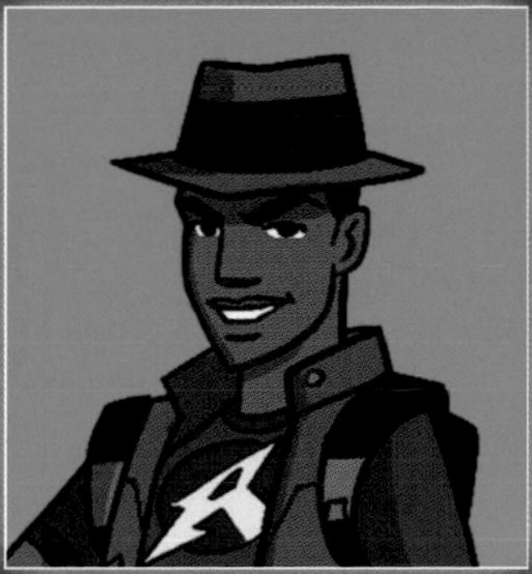

NICK AXIOM

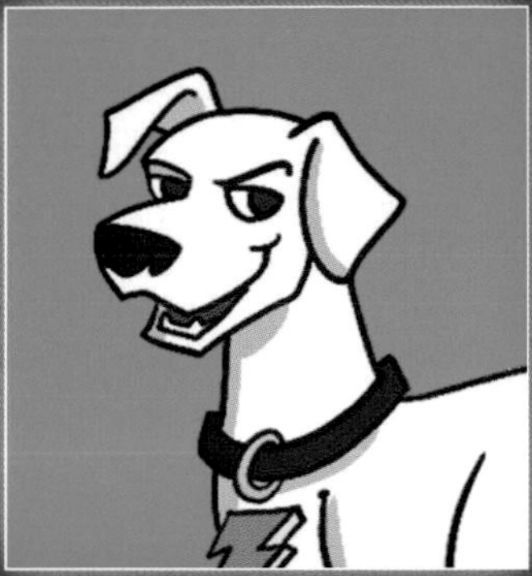

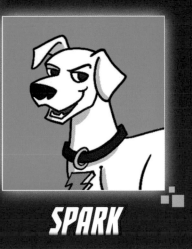

SPARK

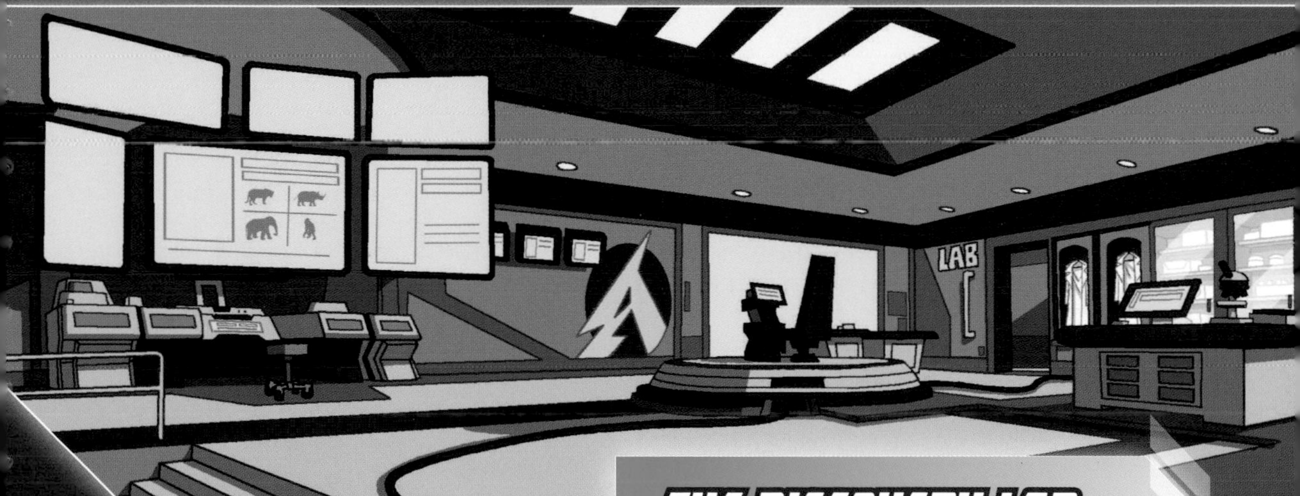
LAB

THE DISCOVERY LAB

Home of the Society of Super Scientists, this state-of-the-art lab houses advanced tools for cutting-edge research and radical scientific innovation. More importantly, it is a space for Super Scientists to collaborate and share knowledge as they work together to tackle any challenge.

SECTION 1: A RAINY RESCUE

When a major storm hits, the Society of Super-Scientists swings into action to help rescue a family from rising floodwaters.

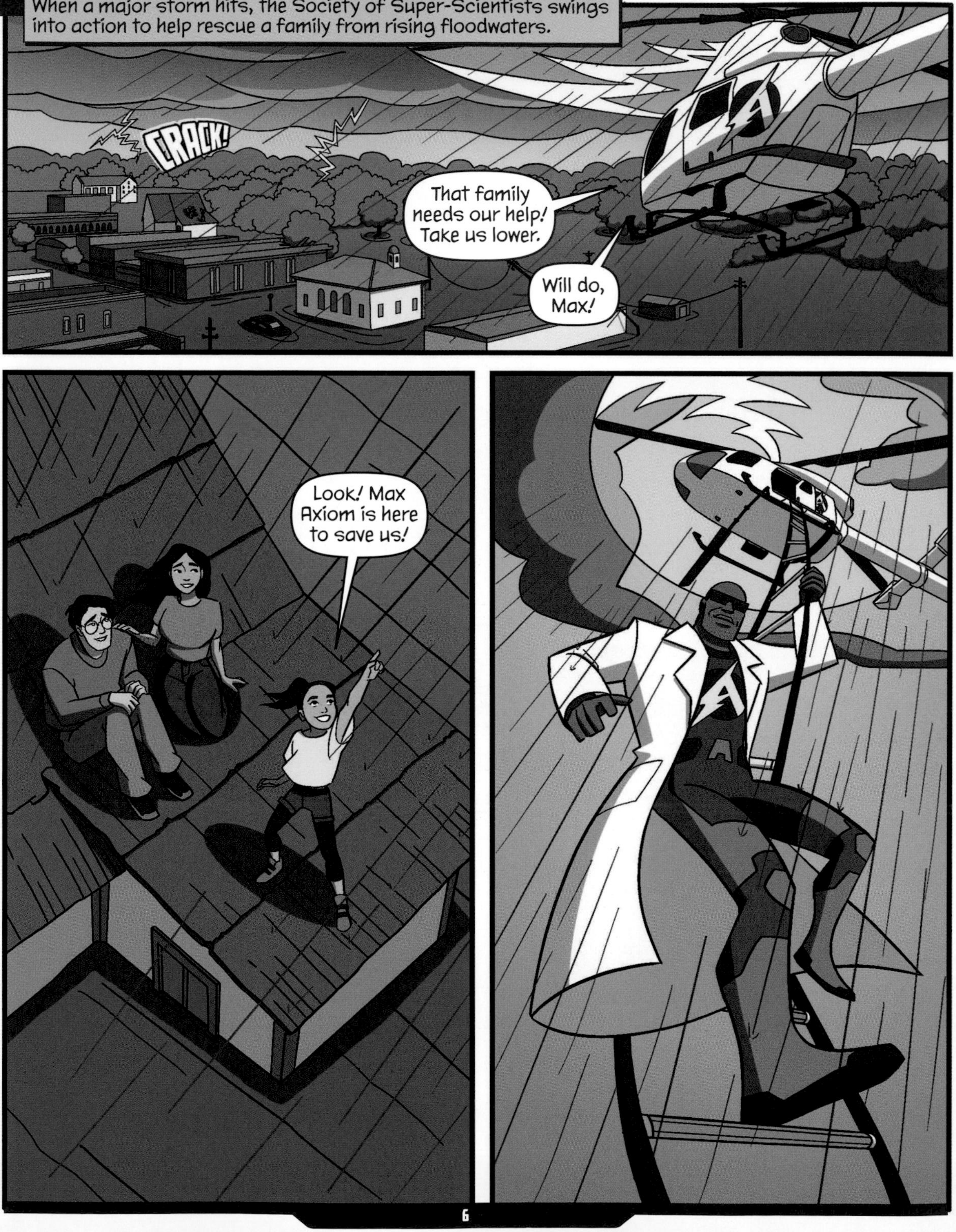

CRACK!
That family needs our help! Take us lower.
Will do, Max!
Look! Max Axiom is here to save us!

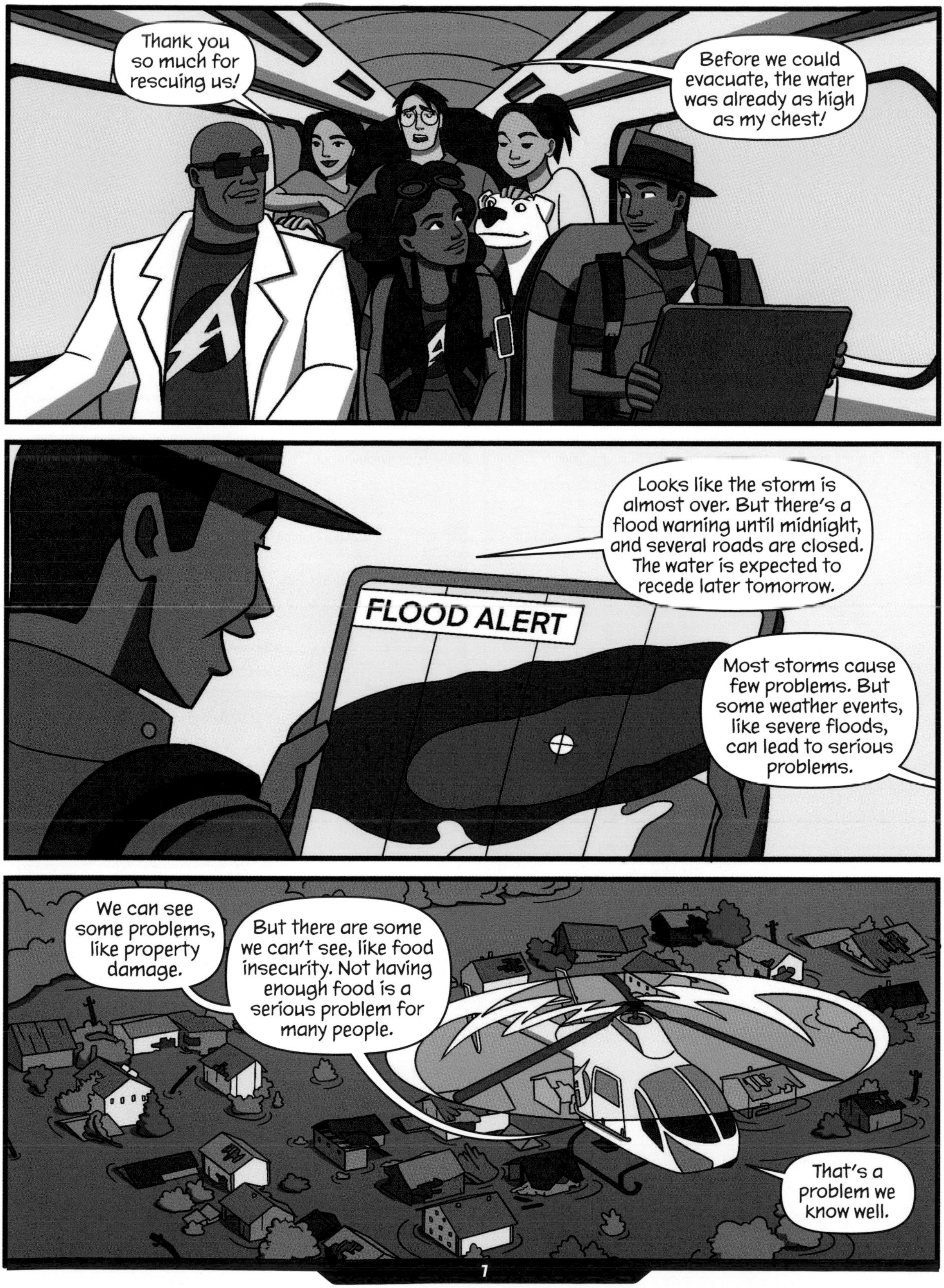

Thank you so much for rescuing us!
Before we could evacuate, the water was already as high as my chest!
Looks like the storm is almost over. But there's a flood warning until midnight, and several roads are closed. The water is expected to recede later tomorrow.
FLOOD ALERT
Most storms cause few problems. But some weather events, like severe floods, can lead to serious problems.
We can see some problems, like property damage.
But there are some we can't see, like food insecurity. Not having enough food is a serious problem for many people.
That's a problem we know well.

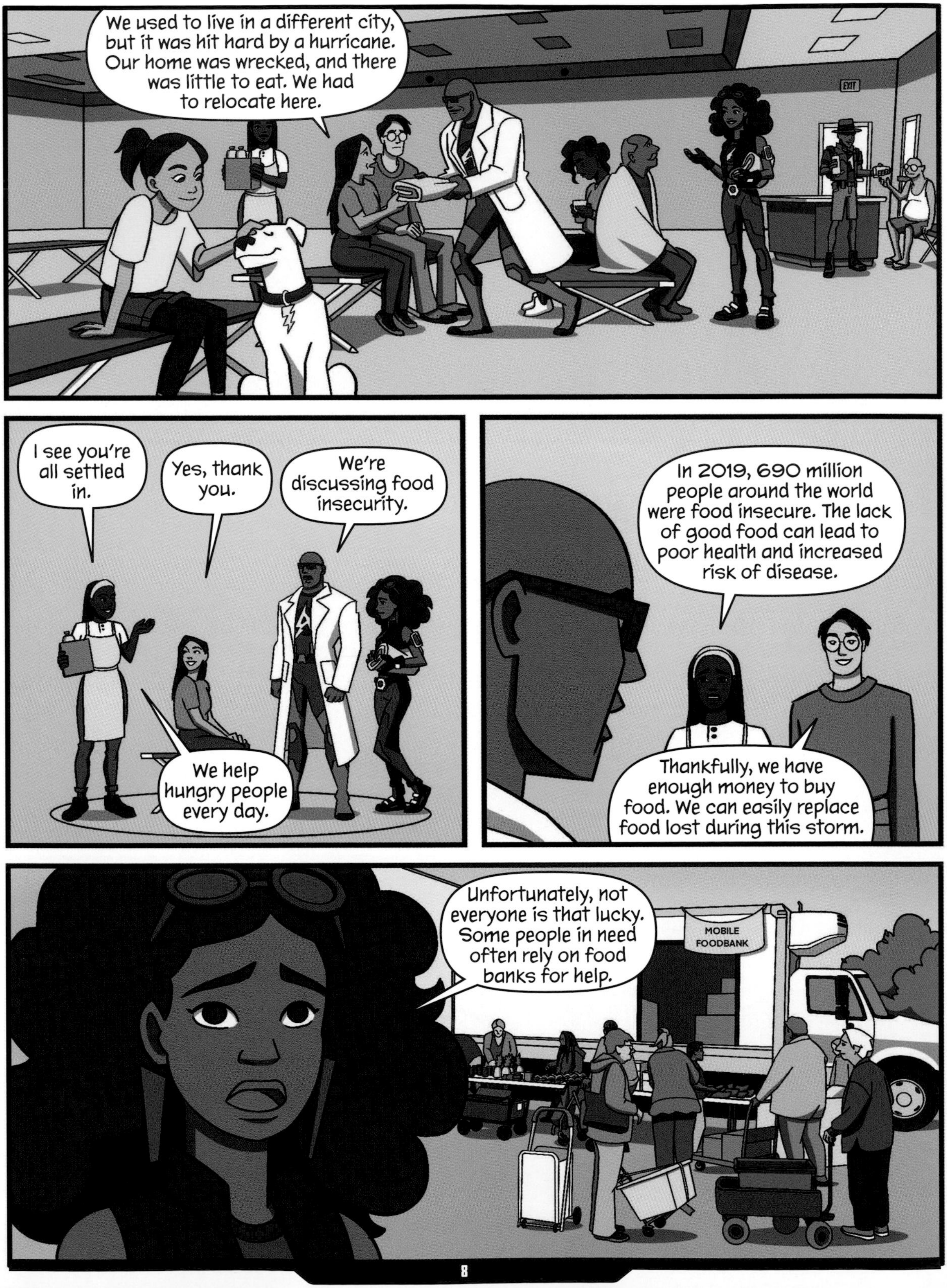

We used to live in a different city, but it was hit hard by a hurricane. Our home was wrecked, and there was little to eat. We had to relocate here.
EXIT
I see you're all settled in.
Yes, thank you.
We're discussing food insecurity.
We help hungry people every day.
In 2019, 690 million people around the world were food insecure. The lack of good food can lead to poor health and increased risk of disease.
Thankfully, we have enough money to buy food. We can easily replace food lost during this storm.
Unfortunately, not everyone is that lucky. Some people in need often rely on food banks for help.
MOBILE FOODBANK

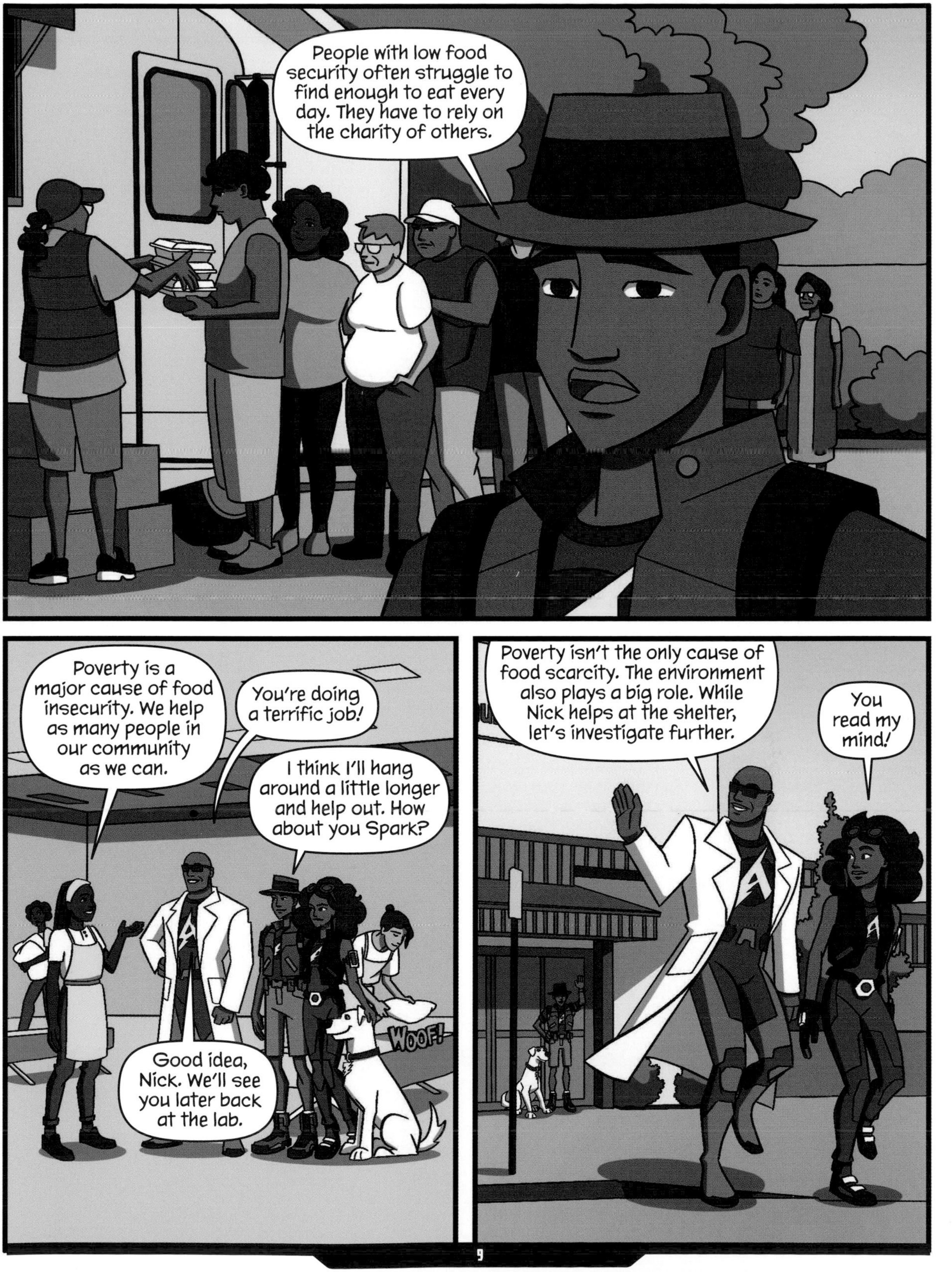
People with low food security often struggle to find enough to eat every day. They have to rely on the charity of others.
Poverty is a major cause of food insecurity. We help as many people in our community as we can.
You're doing a terrific job!
I think I'll hang around a little longer and help out. How about you Spark?
Good idea, Nick. We'll see you later back at the lab.
WOOF!
Poverty isn't the only cause of food scarcity. The environment also plays a big role. While Nick helps at the shelter, let's investigate further.
You read my mind!

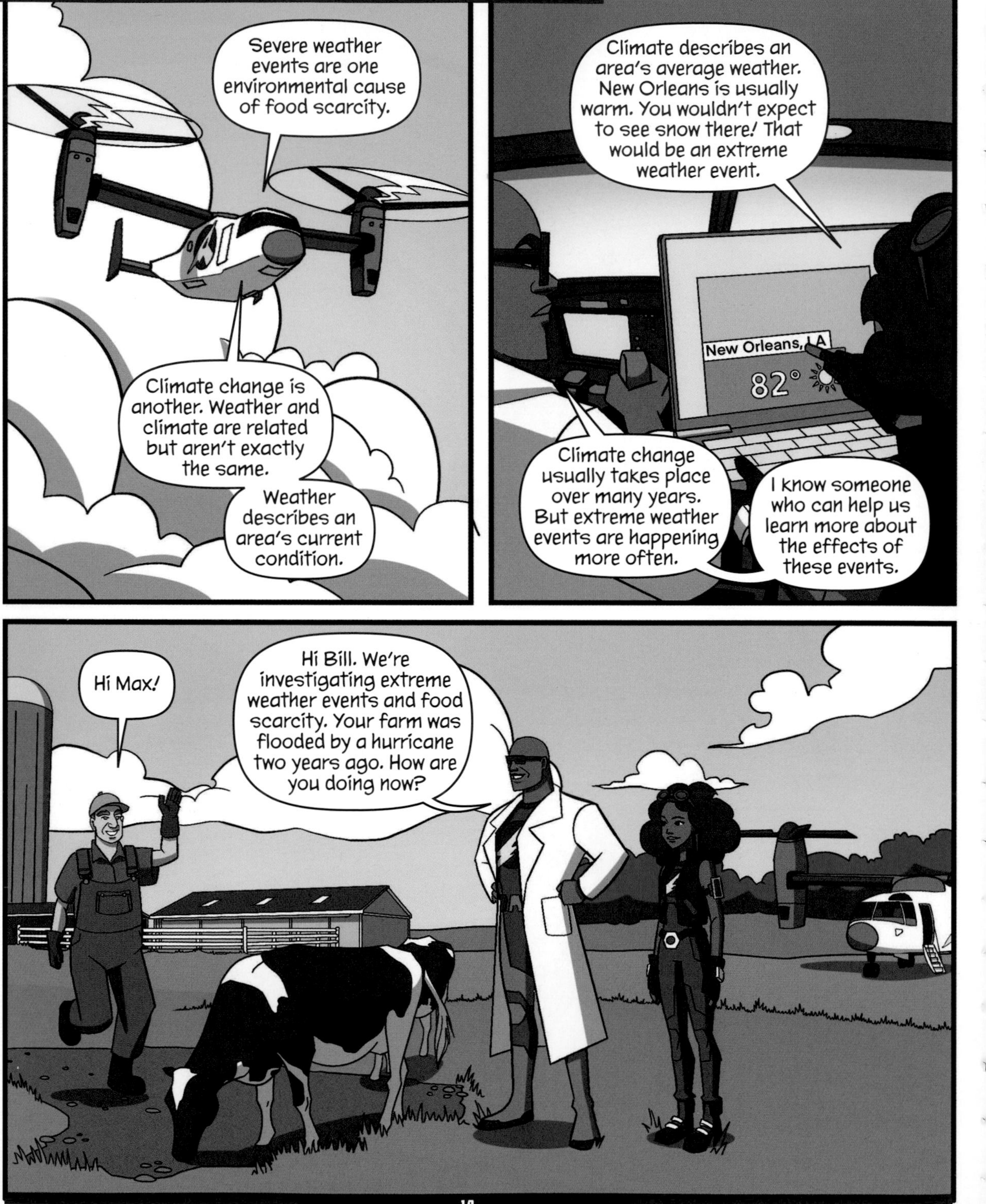
Severe weather events are one environmental cause of food scarcity.
Climate change is another. Weather and climate are related but aren't exactly the same.
Weather describes an area's current condition.
Climate describes an area's average weather. New Orleans is usually warm. You wouldn't expect to see snow there! That would be an extreme weather event.
New Orleans, LA
82°
Climate change usually takes place over many years. But extreme weather events are happening more often.
I know someone who can help us learn more about the effects of these events.
Hi Max!
Hi Bill. We're investigating extreme weather events and food scarcity. Your farm was flooded by a hurricane two years ago. How are you doing now?

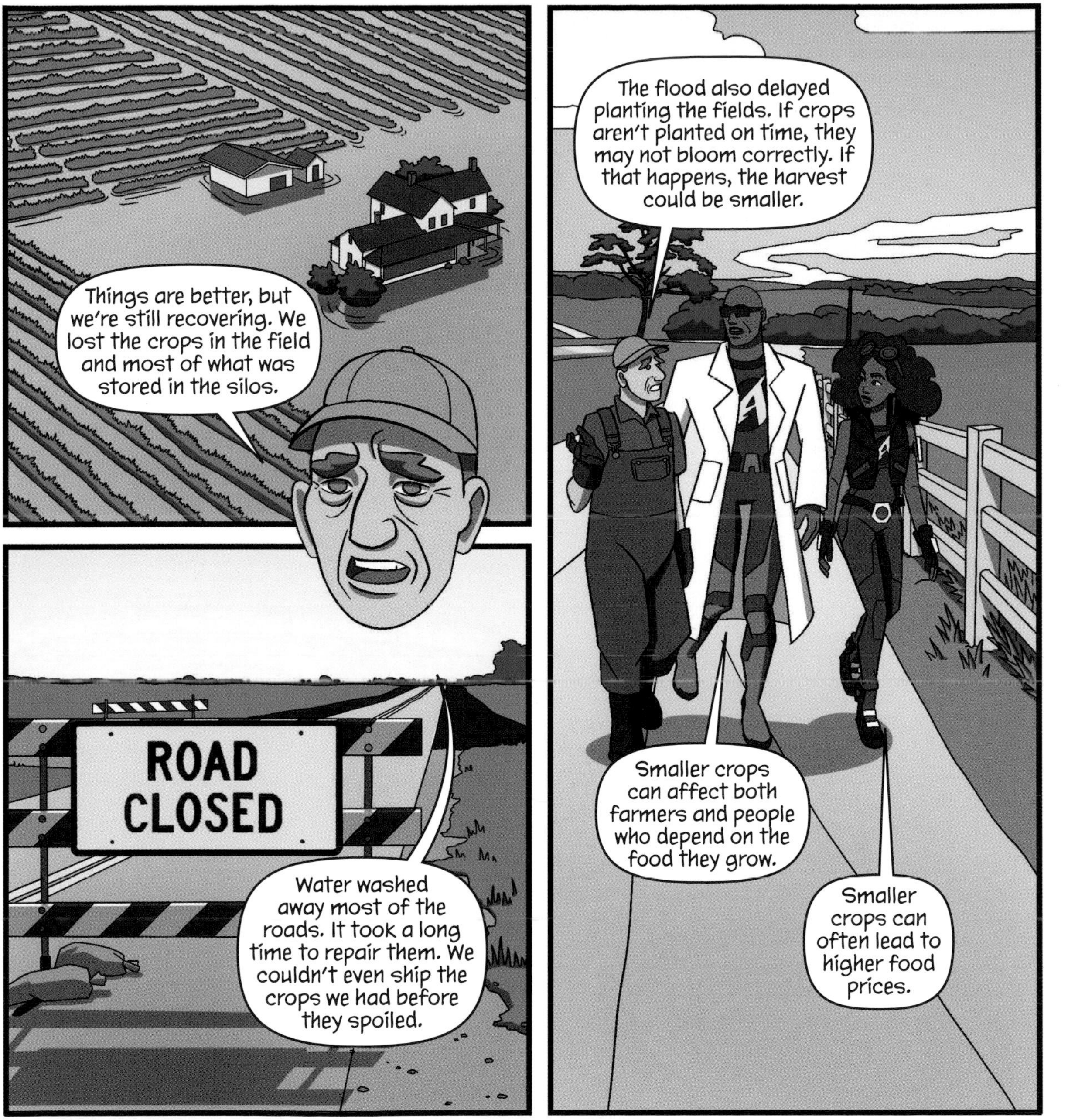
Things are better, but we're still recovering. We lost the crops in the field and most of what was stored in the silos.
ROAD CLOSED
Water washed away most of the roads. It took a long time to repair them. We couldn't even ship the crops we had before they spoiled.
The flood also delayed planting the fields. If crops aren't planted on time, they may not bloom correctly. If that happens, the harvest could be smaller.
Smaller crops can affect both farmers and people who depend on the food they grow.
Smaller crops can often lead to higher food prices.

RETIRING HURRICANE NAMES

Hurricanes often cause major flooding as they travel over land. Before 1953, tropical storms and hurricanes were tracked by the year and order they occurred. Then the United States started giving the storms female names. Male names were added in 1978. If a storm is extremely deadly or costly, its name is retired. Recent retired names include Katrina (2005), Rita (2005), Gustov (2008), Sandy (2012), and Maria (2017).

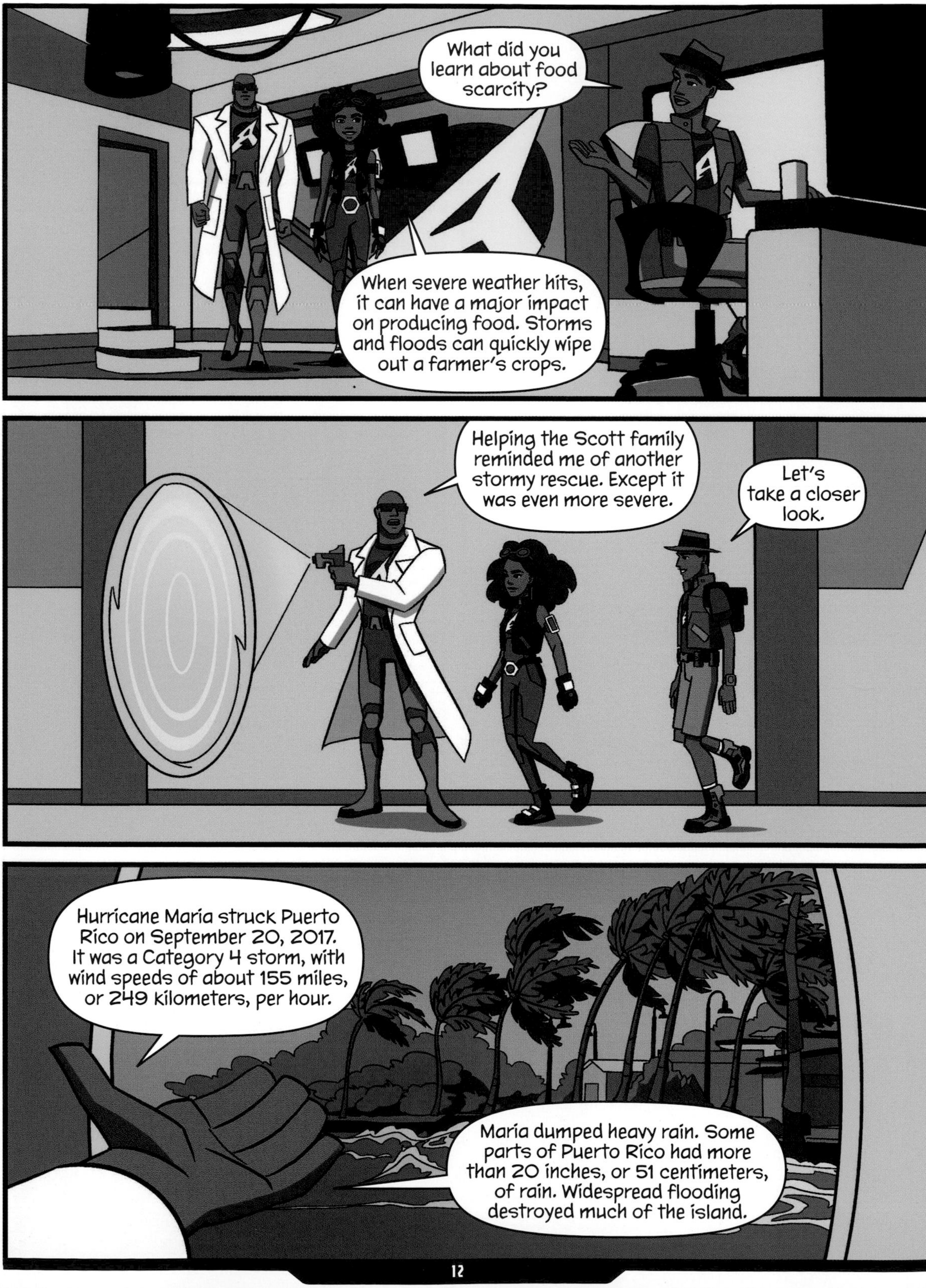
What did you learn about food scarcity?
When severe weather hits, it can have a major impact on producing food. Storms and floods can quickly wipe out a farmer's crops.
Helping the Scott family reminded me of another stormy rescue. Except it was even more severe.
Let's take a closer look.
Hurricane Maria struck Puerto Rico on September 20, 2017. It was a Category 4 storm, with wind speeds of about 155 miles, or 249 kilometers, per hour.
Maria dumped heavy rain. Some parts of Puerto Rico had more than 20 inches, or 51 centimeters, of rain. Widespread flooding destroyed much of the island.

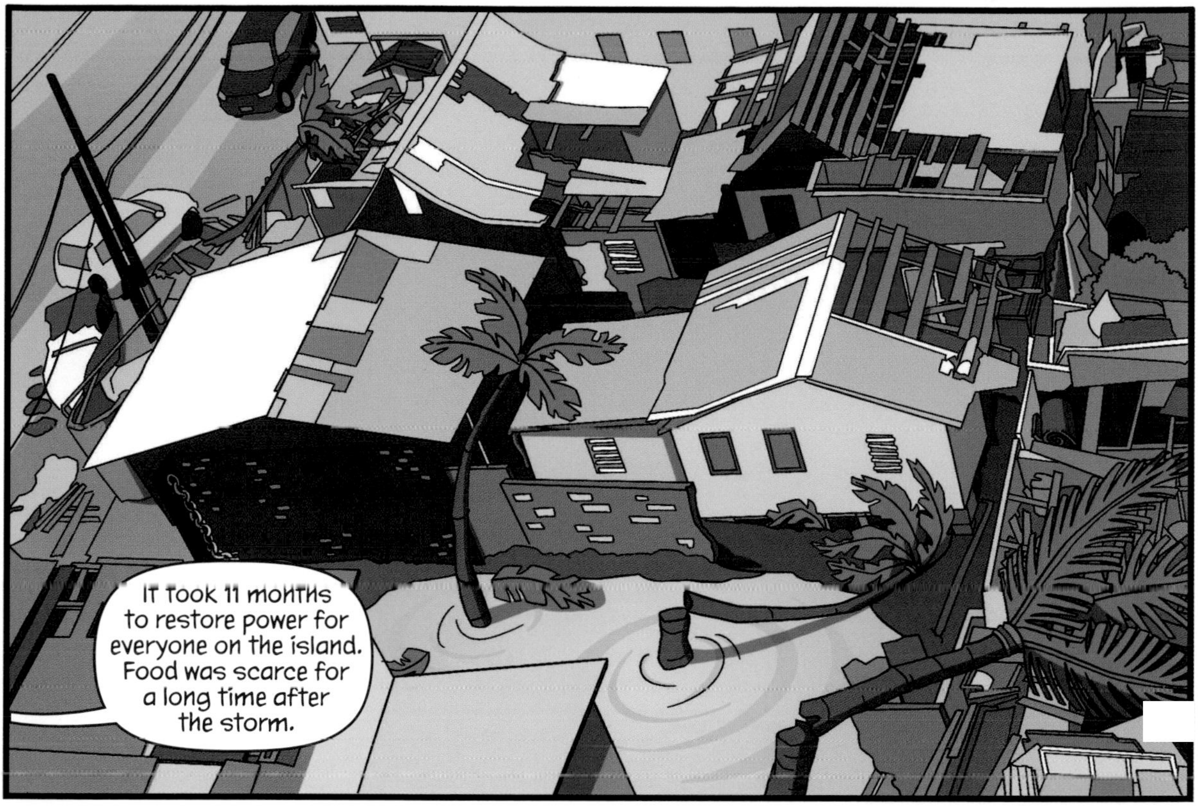
IT TOOK 11 MONTHS to restore power for everyone on the island. Food was scarce for a long time after the storm.

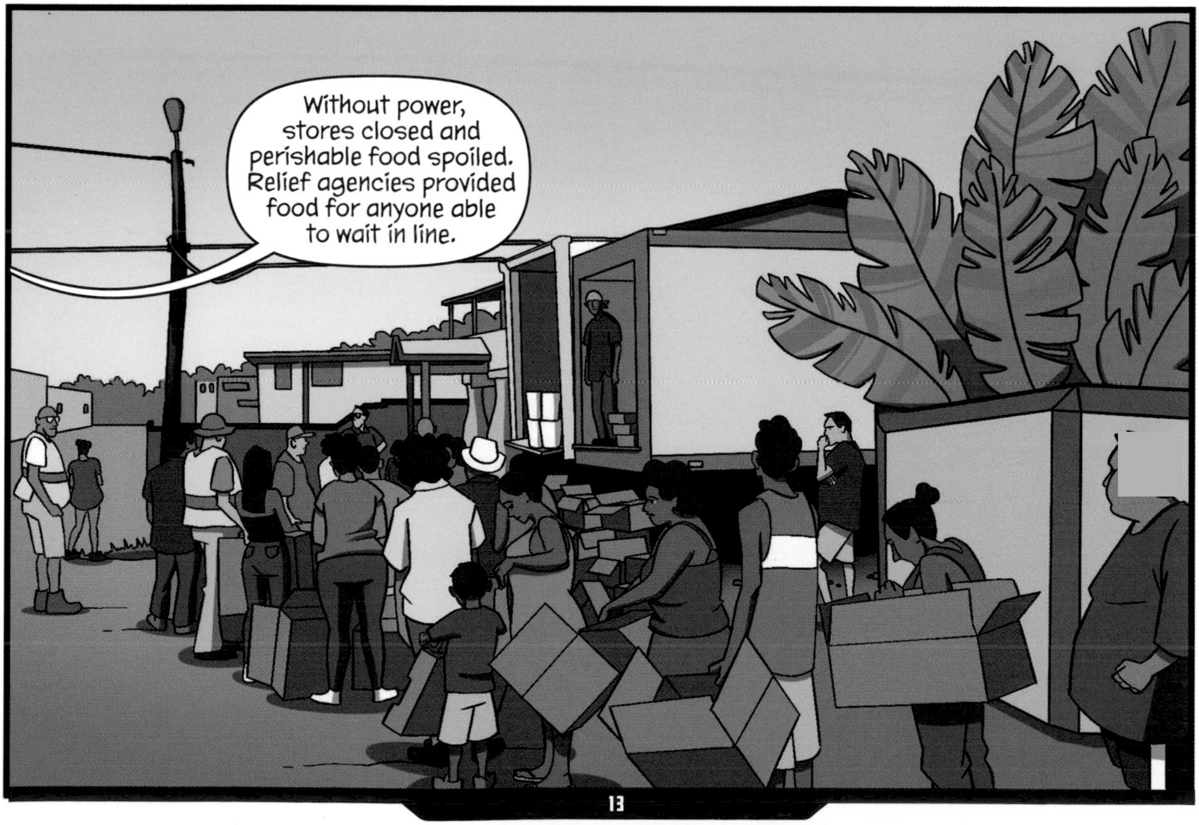
Without power, stores closed and perishable food spoiled. Relief agencies provided food for anyone able to wait in line.

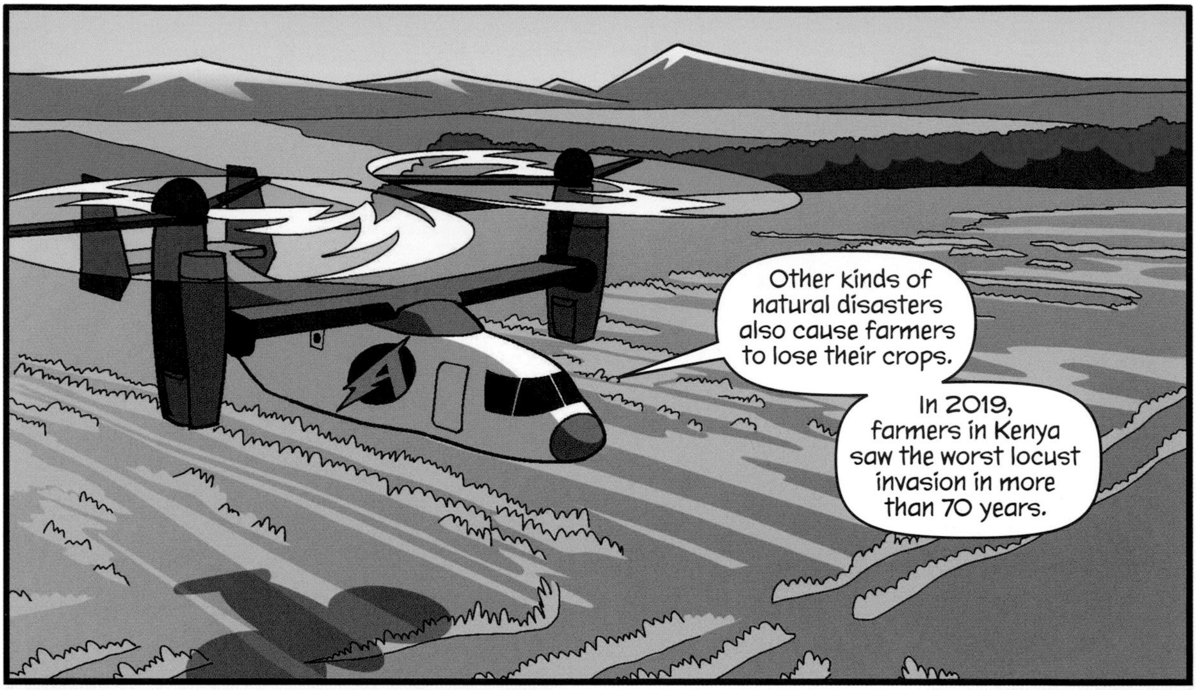
Other kinds of natural disasters also cause farmers to lose their crops.
In 2019, farmers in Kenya saw the worst locust invasion in more than 70 years.

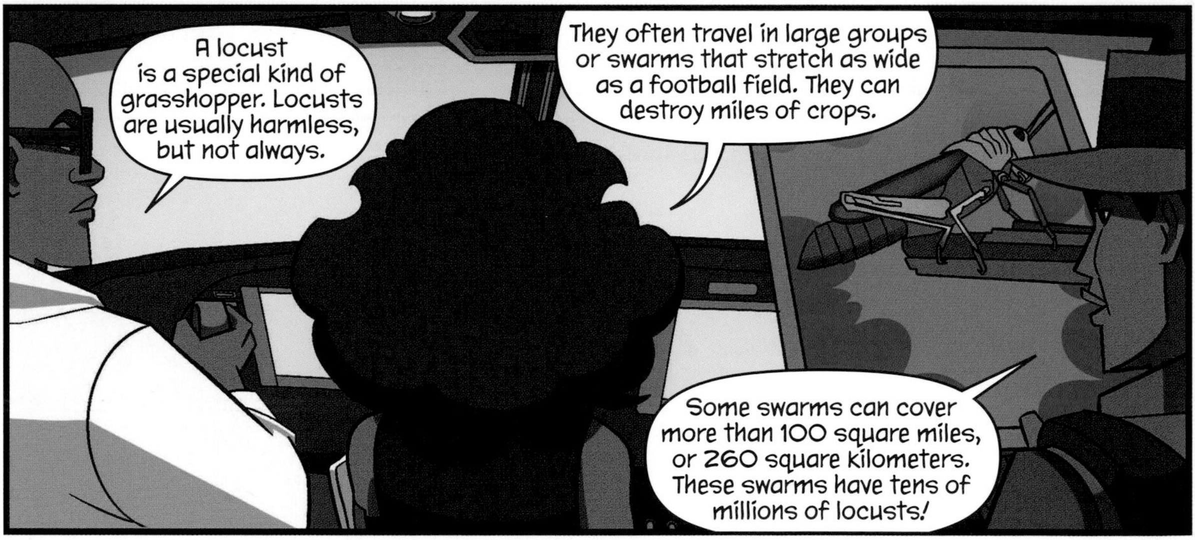
A locust is a special kind of grasshopper. Locusts are usually harmless, but not always.
They often travel in large groups or swarms that stretch as wide as a football field. They can destroy miles of crops.
Some swarms can cover more than 100 square miles, or 260 square kilometers. These swarms have tens of millions of locusts!

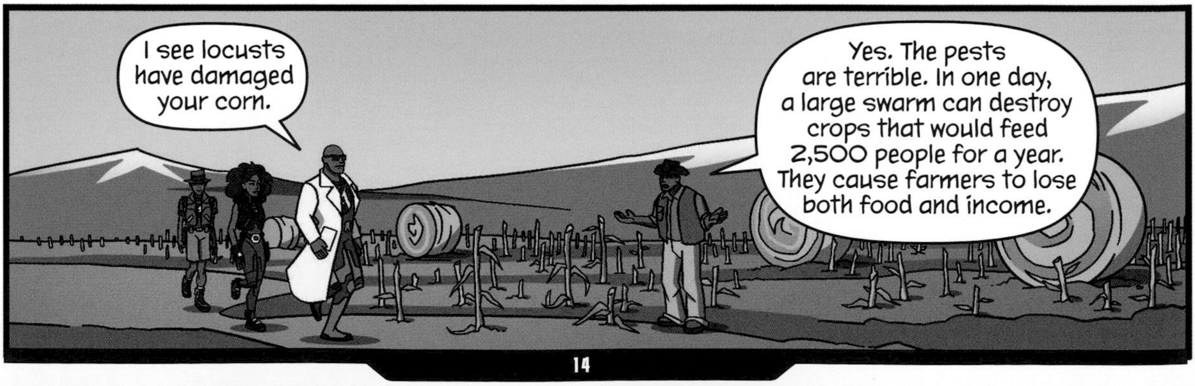
I see locusts have damaged your corn.
Yes. The pests are terrible. In one day, a large swarm can destroy crops that would feed 2,500 people for a year. They cause farmers to lose both food and income.

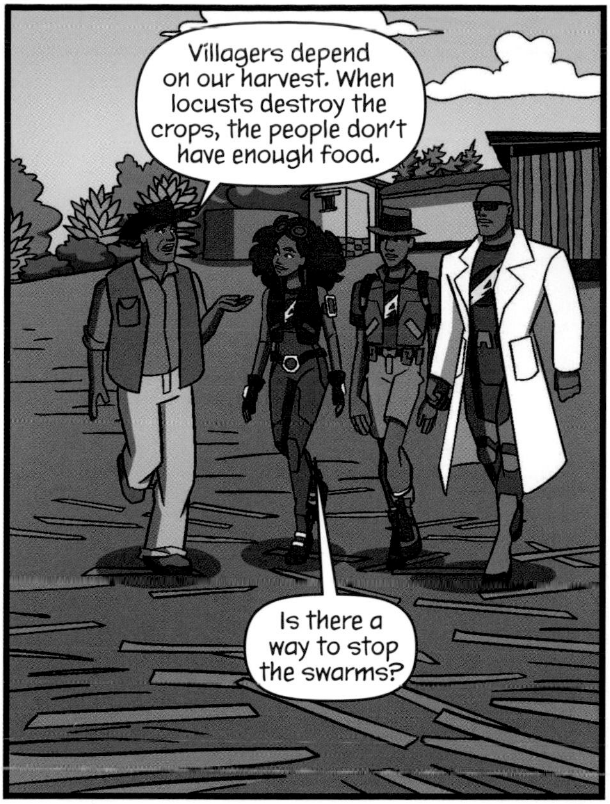
Villagers depend on our harvest. When locusts destroy the crops, the people don't have enough food.
Is there a way to stop the swarms?

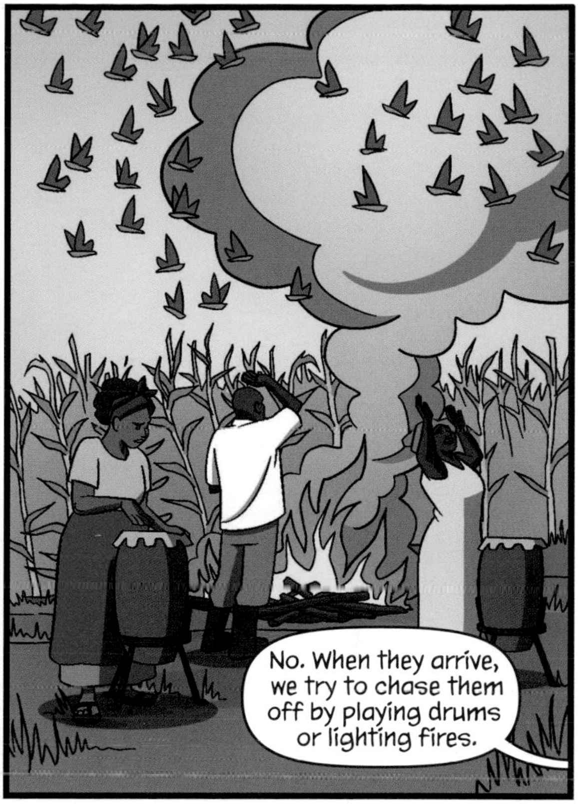
No. When they arrive, we try to chase them off by playing drums or lighting fires.

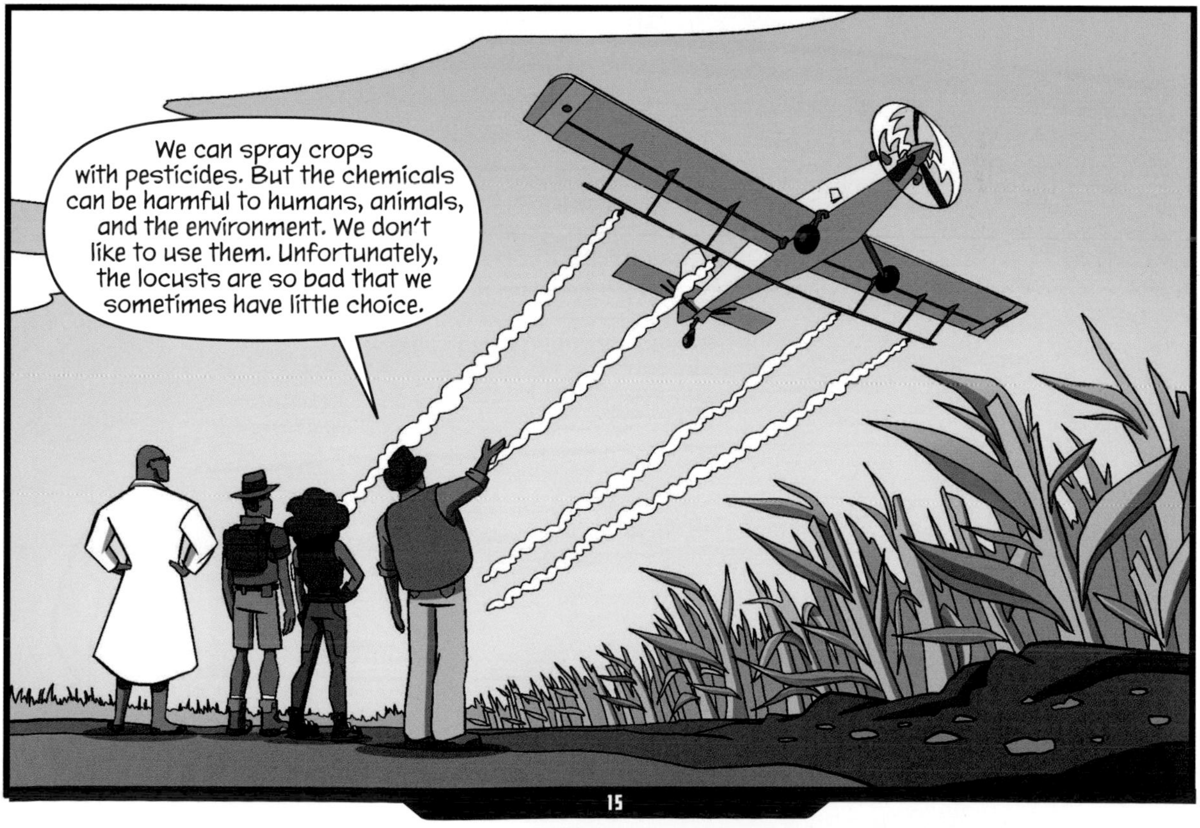
We can spray crops with pesticides. But the chemicals can be harmful to humans, animals, and the environment. We don't like to use them. Unfortunately, the locusts are so bad that we sometimes have little choice.

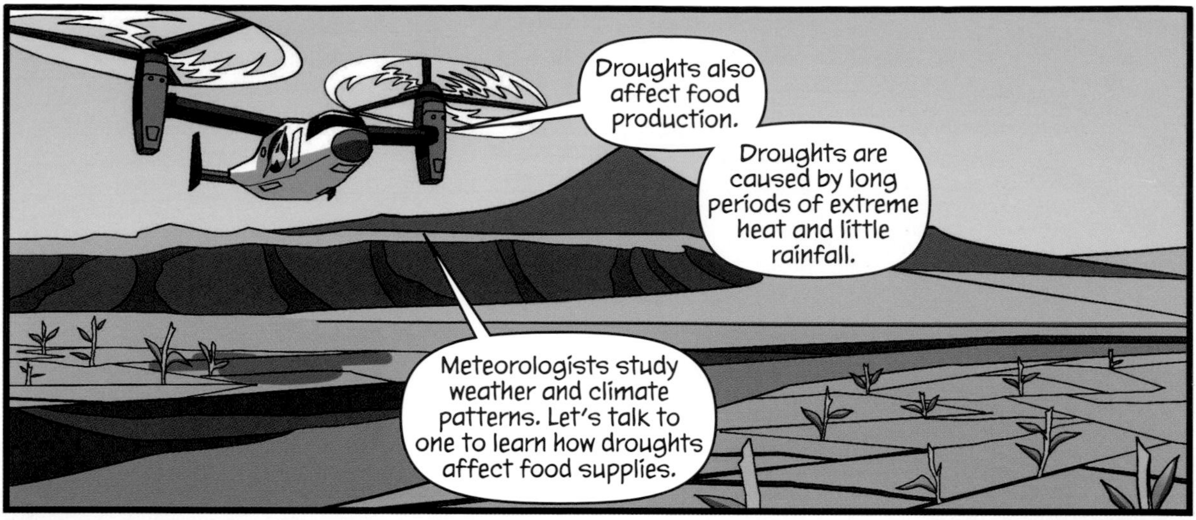
Droughts also affect food production.
Droughts are caused by long periods of extreme heat and little rainfall.
Meteorologists study weather and climate patterns. Let's talk to one to learn how droughts affect food supplies.

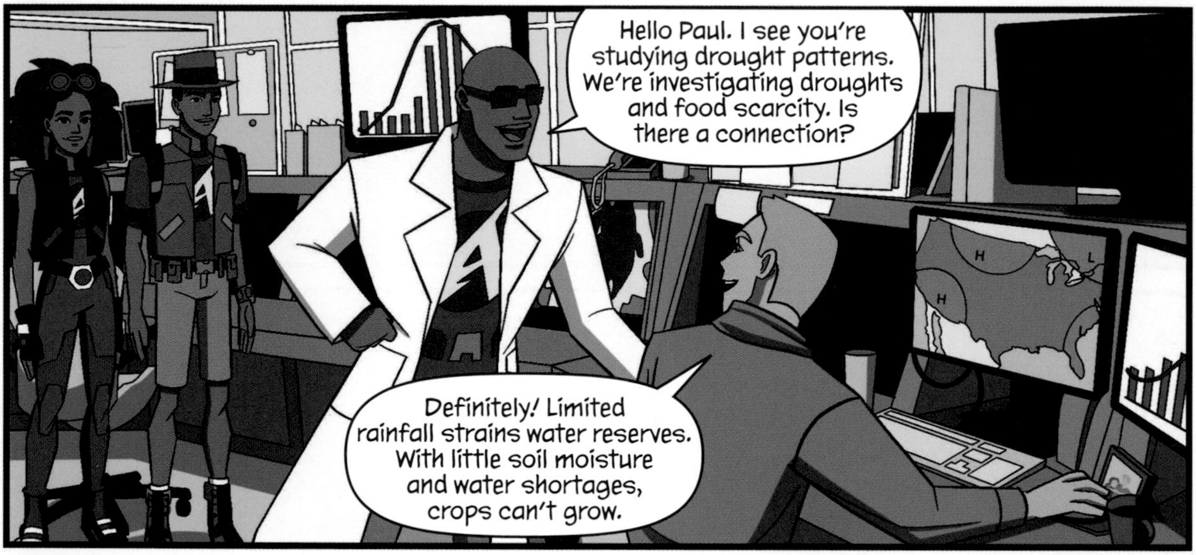
Hello Paul. I see you're studying drought patterns. We're investigating droughts and food scarcity. Is there a connection?
Definitely! Limited rainfall strains water reserves. With little soil moisture and water shortages, crops can't grow.

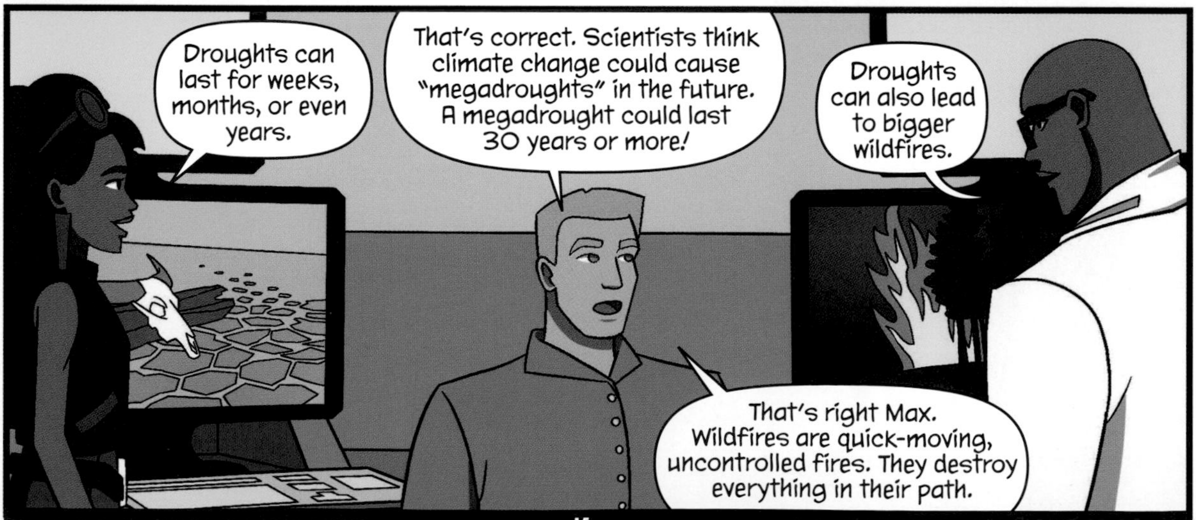
Droughts can last for weeks, months, or even years.
That's correct. Scientists think climate change could cause "megadroughts" in the future. A megadrought could last 30 years or more!
Droughts can also lead to bigger wildfires.
That's right Max. Wildfires are quick-moving, uncontrolled fires. They destroy everything in their path.

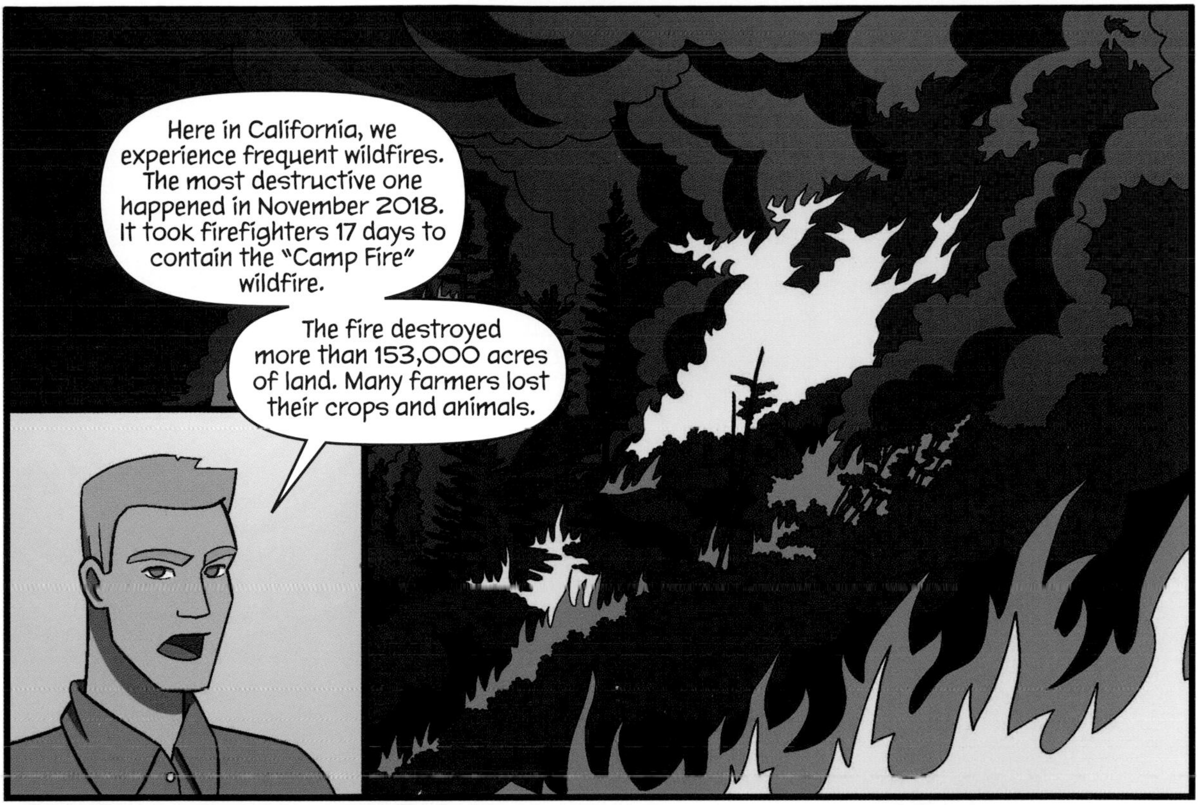
Here in California, we experience frequent wildfires. The most destructive one happened in November 2018. It took firefighters 17 days to contain the "Camp Fire" wildfire.
The fire destroyed more than 153,000 acres of land. Many farmers lost their crops and animals.

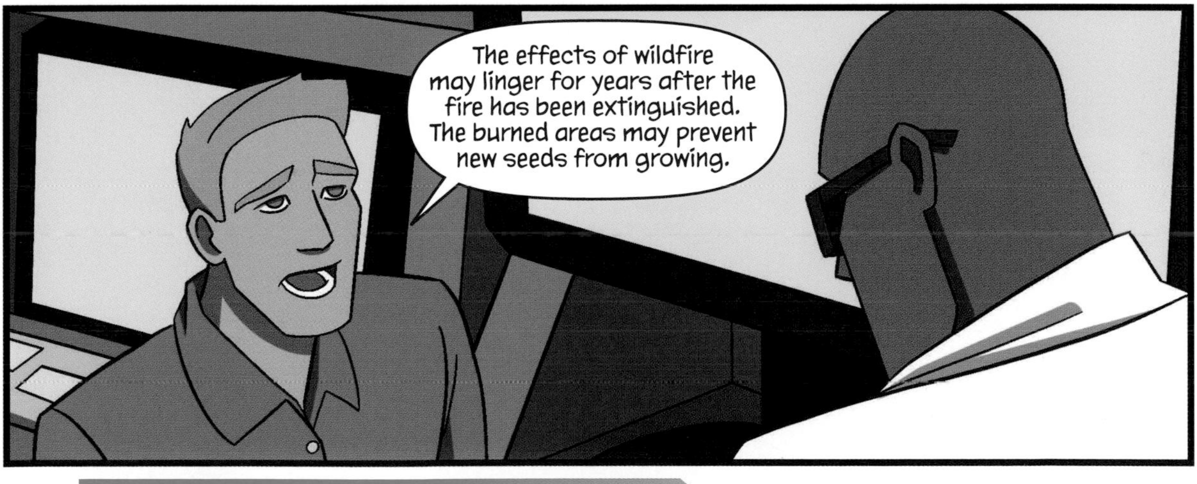
The effects of wildfire may linger for years after the fire has been extinguished. The burned areas may prevent new seeds from growing.

WARS AND FOOD SCARCITY

Long-lasting wars and conflicts often cause food shortages. Soldiers sometimes steal or destroy food supplies to damage their enemies. They ruin farms and kill livestock. Conflicts can keep farmers from getting new seed or watering their crops, which causes delays and slows down food production. Even if farmers have a good harvest, they may not be able to sell their crops. During wartime, people can go hungry for months or years.

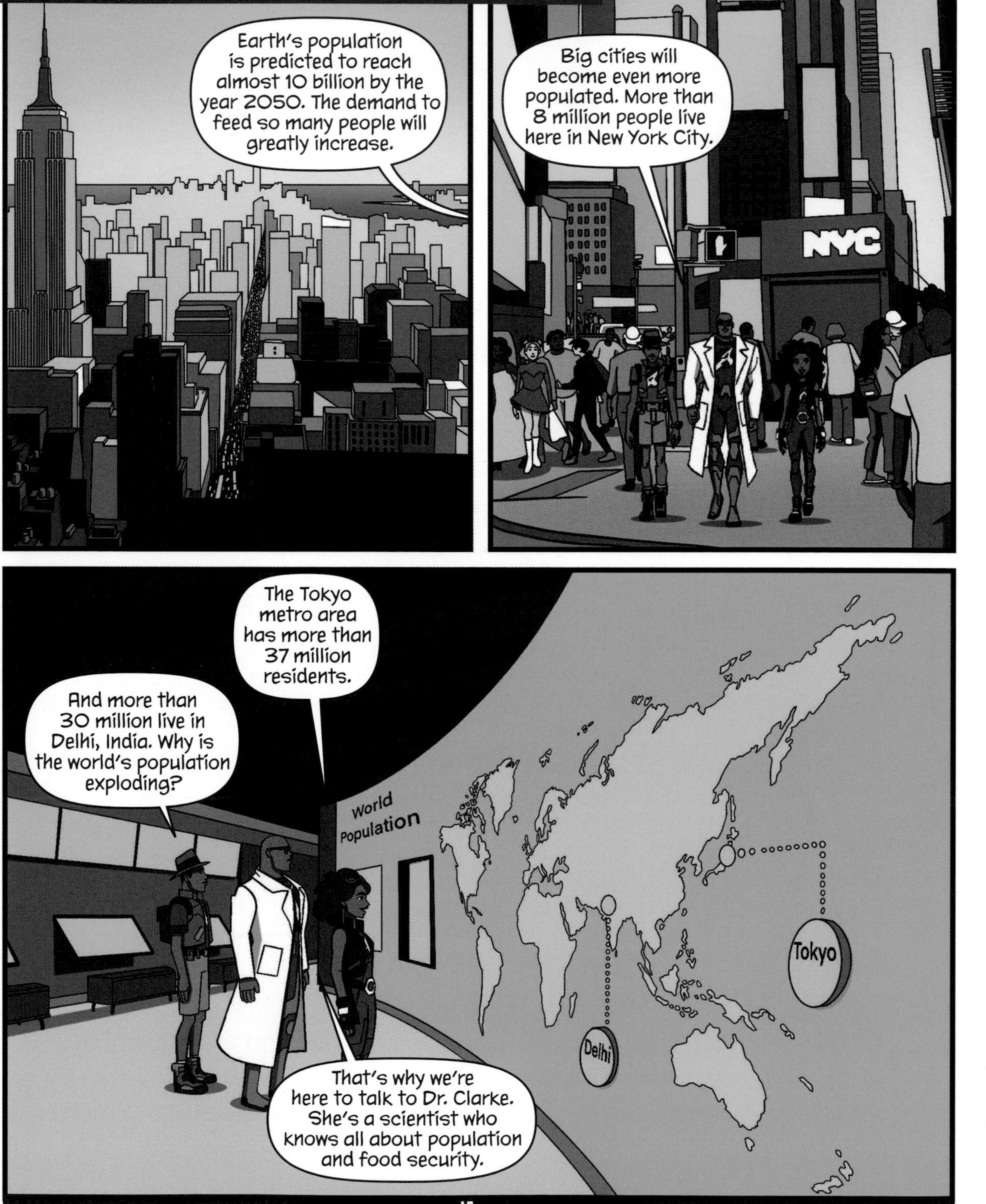
Earth's population is predicted to reach almost 10 billion by the year 2050. The demand to feed so many people will greatly increase.
Big cities will become even more populated. More than 8 million people live here in New York City.
NYC
The Tokyo metro area has more than 37 million residents.
And more than 30 million live in Delhi, India. Why is the world's population exploding?
World Population
Tokyo
Delhi
That's why we're here to talk to Dr. Clarke. She's a scientist who knows all about population and food security.

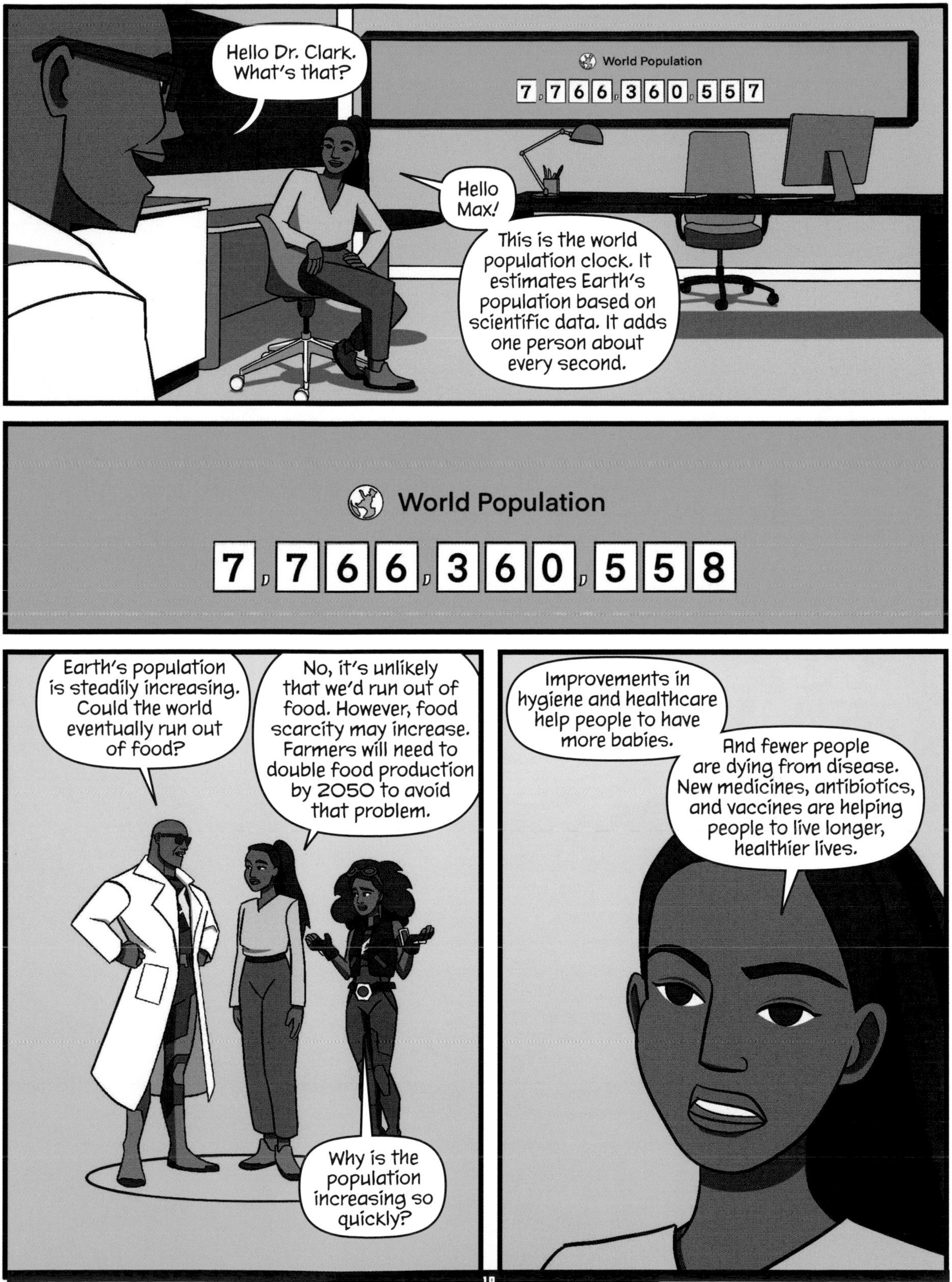

Hello Dr. Clark. What's that?
World Population
7,766,360,557
Hello Max!
This is the world population clock. It estimates Earth's population based on scientific data. It adds one person about every second.
World Population
7,766,360,558
Earth's population is steadily increasing. Could the world eventually run out of food?
No, it's unlikely that we'd run out of food. However, food scarcity may increase. Farmers will need to double food production by 2050 to avoid that problem.
Why is the population increasing so quickly?
Improvements in hygiene and healthcare help people to have more babies.
And fewer people are dying from disease. New medicines, antibiotics, and vaccines are helping people to live longer, healthier lives.

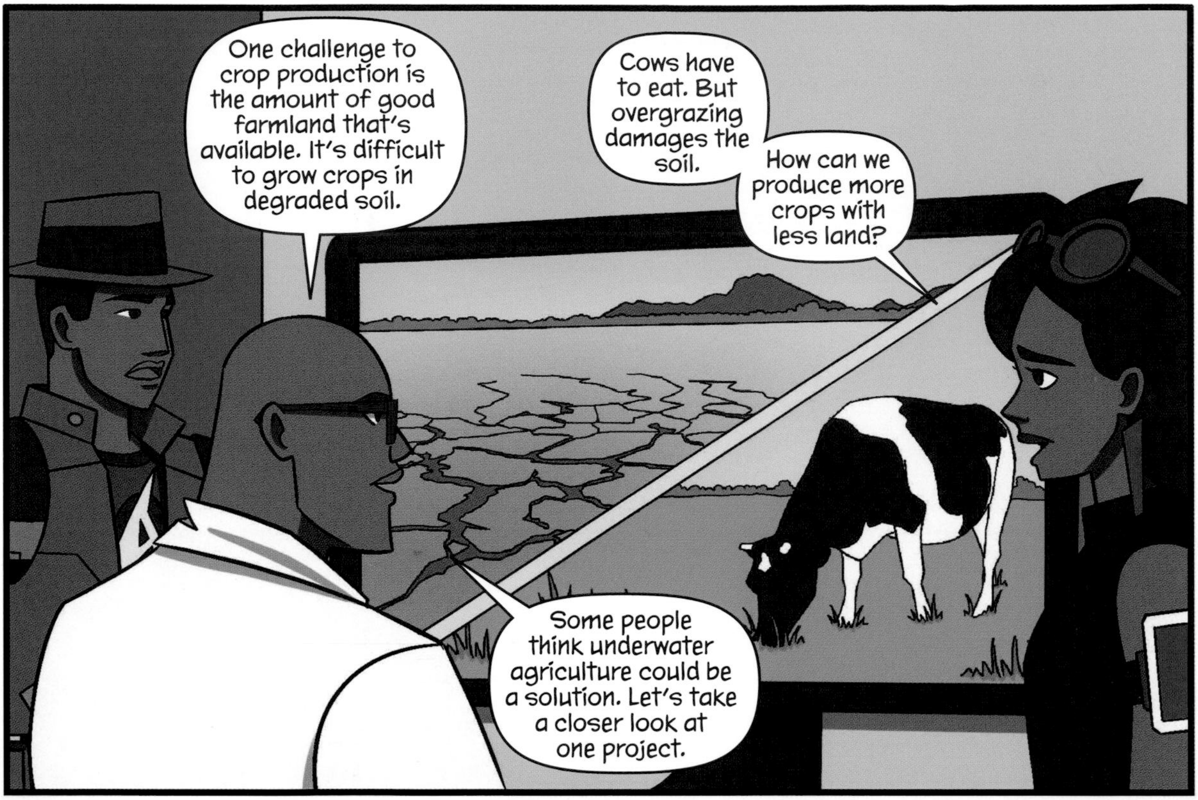
One challenge to crop production is the amount of good farmland that's available. It's difficult to grow crops in degraded soil.
Cows have to eat. But overgrazing damages the soil.
How can we produce more crops with less land?
Some people think underwater agriculture could be a solution. Let's take a closer look at one project.

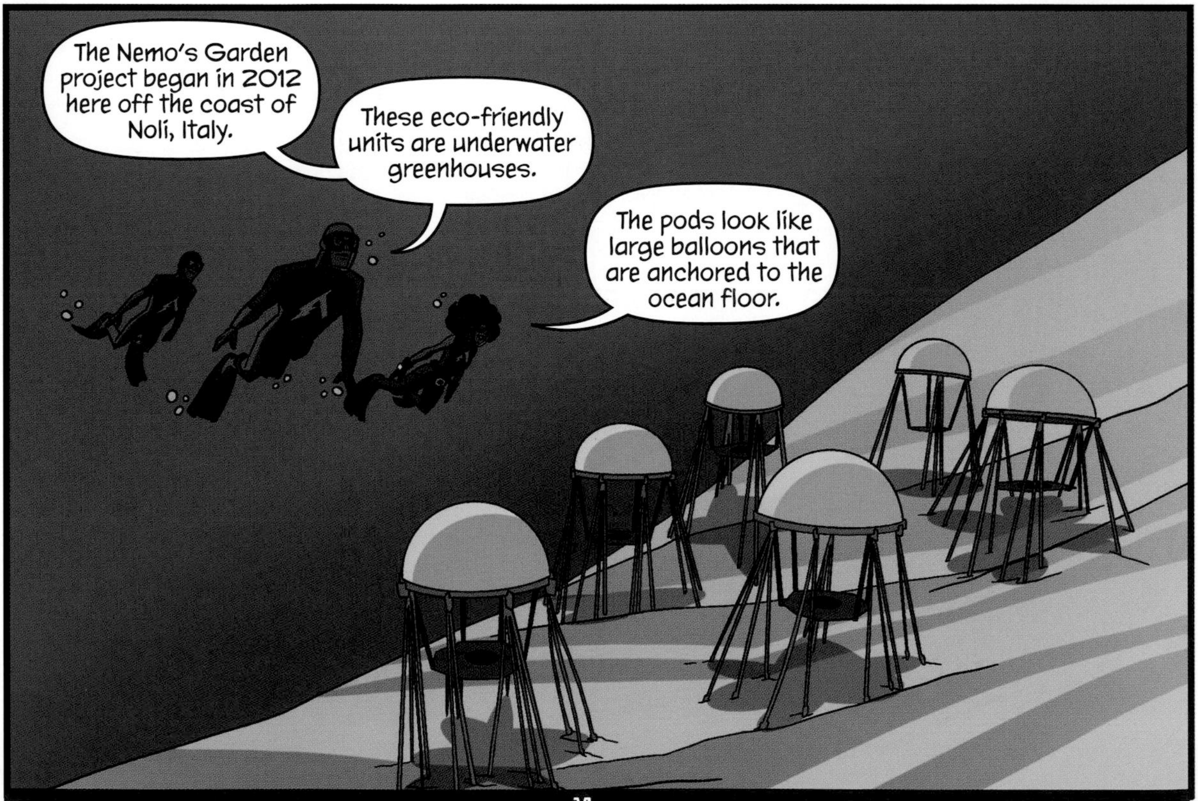
The Nemo's Garden project began in 2012 here off the coast of Noli, Italy.
These eco-friendly units are underwater greenhouses.
The pods look like large balloons that are anchored to the ocean floor.

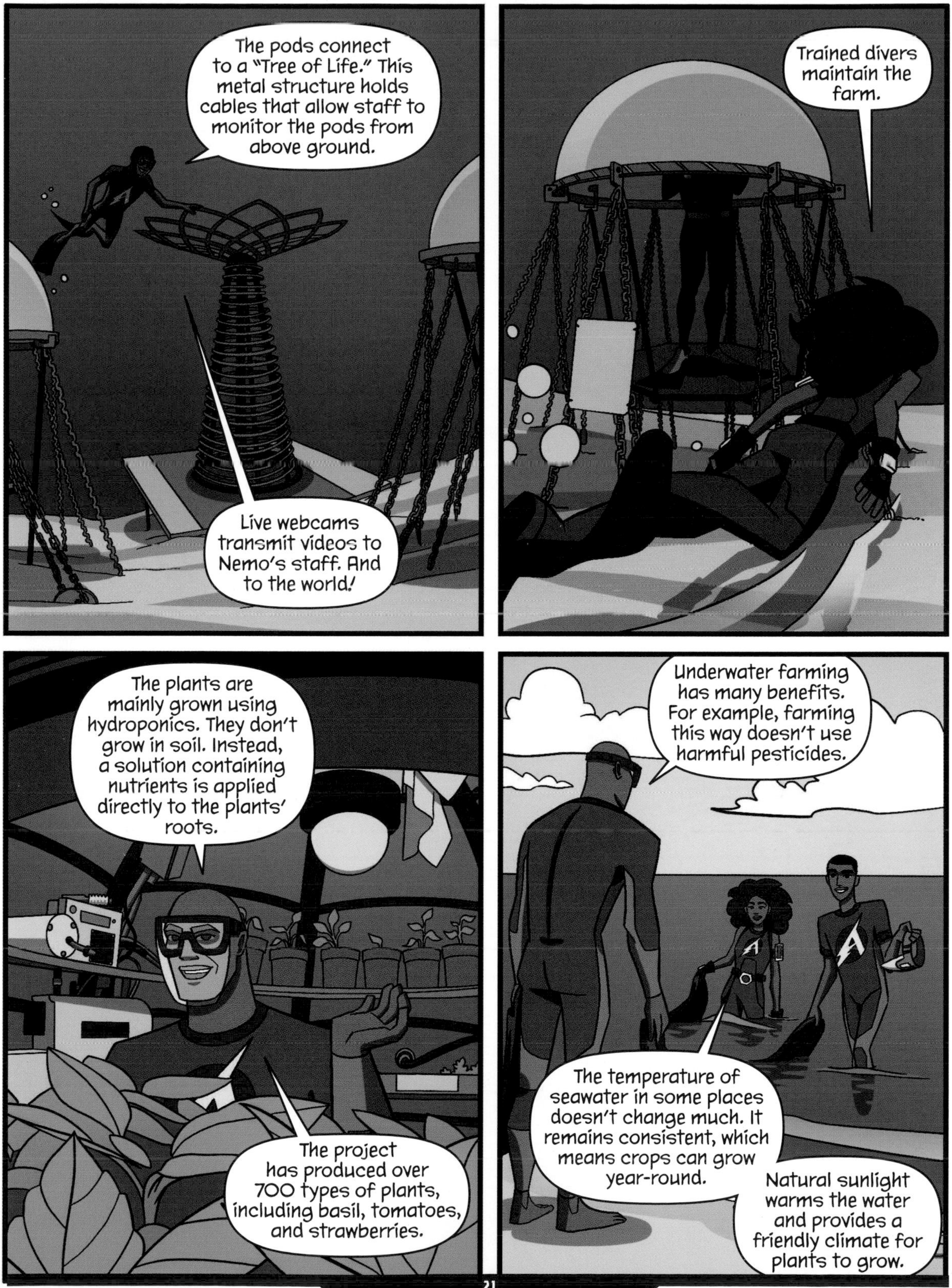
The pods connect to a "Tree of Life." This metal structure holds cables that allow staff to monitor the pods from above ground.
Live webcams transmit videos to Nemo's staff. And to the world!
Trained divers maintain the farm.
The plants are mainly grown using hydroponics. They don't grow in soil. Instead, a solution containing nutrients is applied directly to the plants' roots.
The project has produced over 700 types of plants, including basil, tomatoes, and strawberries.
Underwater farming has many benefits. For example, farming this way doesn't use harmful pesticides.
The temperature of seawater in some places doesn't change much. It remains consistent, which means crops can grow year-round.
Natural sunlight warms the water and provides a friendly climate for plants to grow.

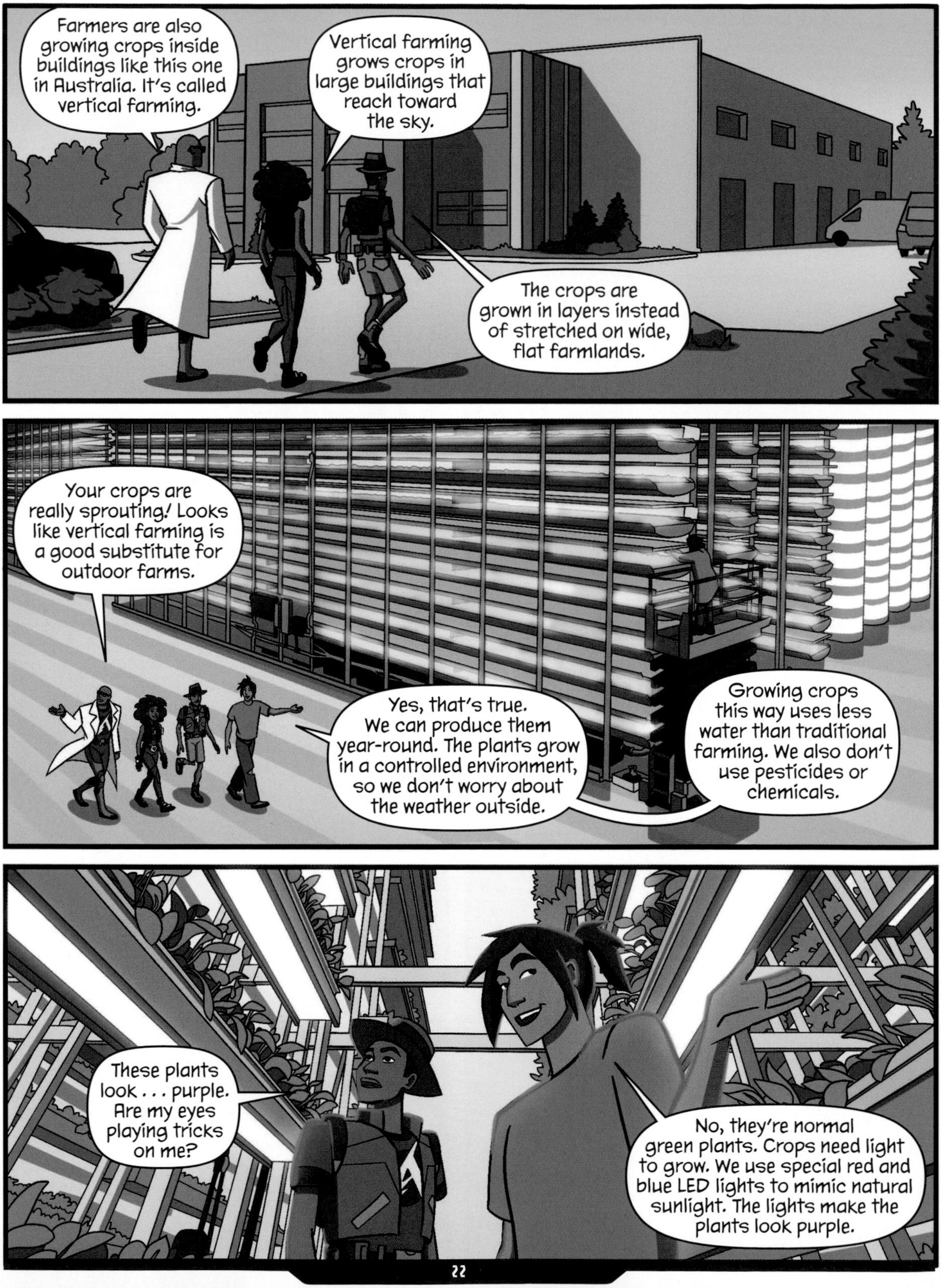
Farmers are also growing crops inside buildings like this one in Australia. It's called vertical farming.
Vertical farming grows crops in large buildings that reach toward the sky.
The crops are grown in layers instead of stretched on wide, flat farmlands.
Your crops are really sprouting! Looks like vertical farming is a good substitute for outdoor farms.
Yes, that's true. We can produce them year-round. The plants grow in a controlled environment, so we don't worry about the weather outside.
Growing crops this way uses less water than traditional farming. We also don't use pesticides or chemicals.
These plants look . . . purple. Are my eyes playing tricks on me?
No, they're normal green plants. Crops need light to grow. We use special red and blue LED lights to mimic natural sunlight. The lights make the plants look purple.

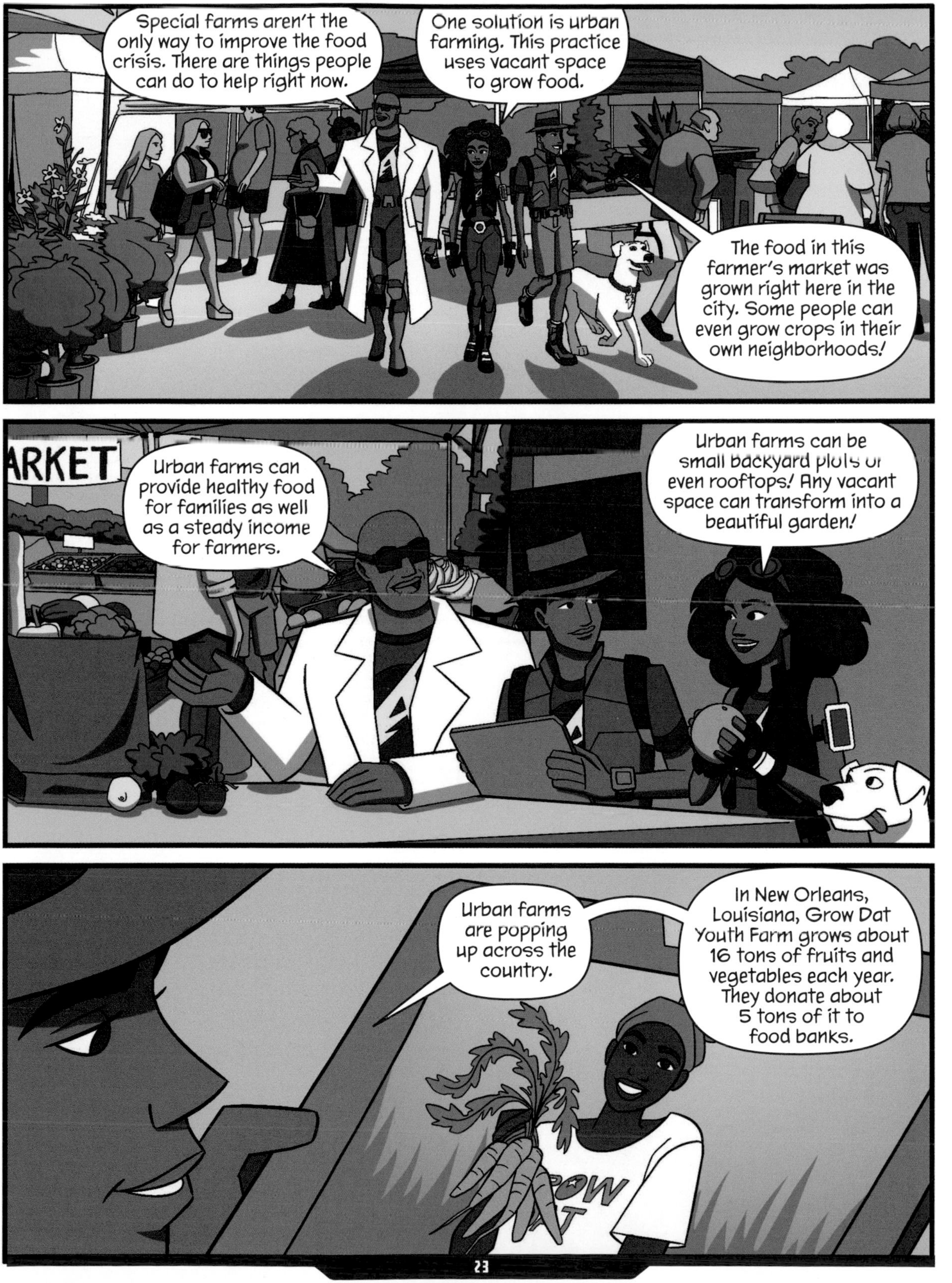
Special farms aren't the only way to improve the food crisis. There are things people can do to help right now.
One solution is urban farming. This practice uses vacant space to grow food.
The food in this farmer's market was grown right here in the city. Some people can even grow crops in their own neighborhoods!
ARKET
Urban farms can provide healthy food for families as well as a steady income for farmers.
Urban farms can be small backyard plots or even rooftops! Any vacant space can transform into a beautiful garden!
Urban farms are popping up across the country.
In New Orleans, Louisiana, Grow Dat Youth Farm grows about 16 tons of fruits and vegetables each year. They donate about 5 tons of it to food banks.

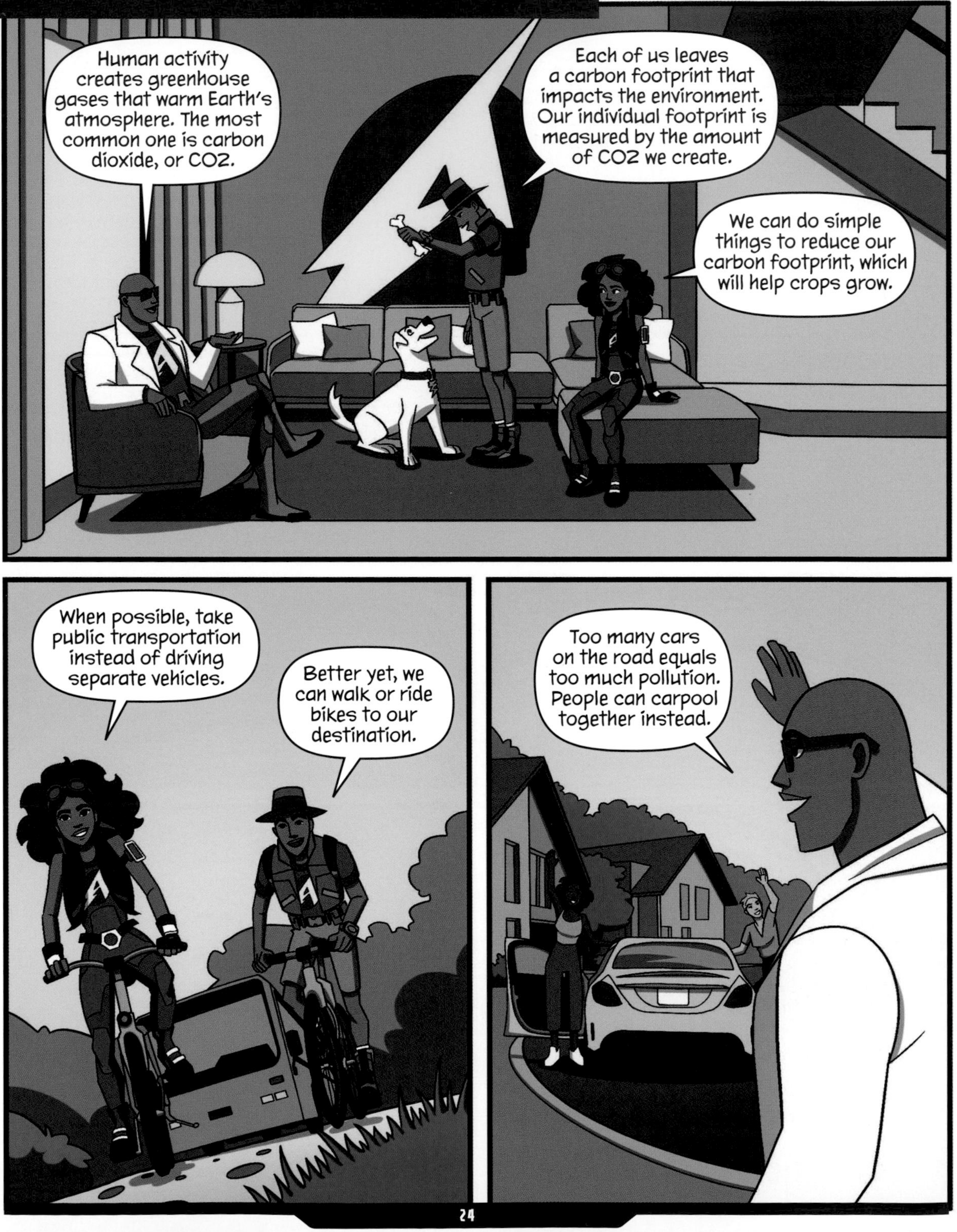
Human activity creates greenhouse gases that warm Earth's atmosphere. The most common one is carbon dioxide, or CO2.
Each of us leaves a carbon footprint that impacts the environment. Our individual footprint is measured by the amount of CO2 we create.
We can do simple things to reduce our carbon footprint, which will help crops grow.
When possible, take public transportation instead of driving separate vehicles.
Better yet, we can walk or ride bikes to our destination.
Too many cars on the road equals too much pollution. People can carpool together instead.

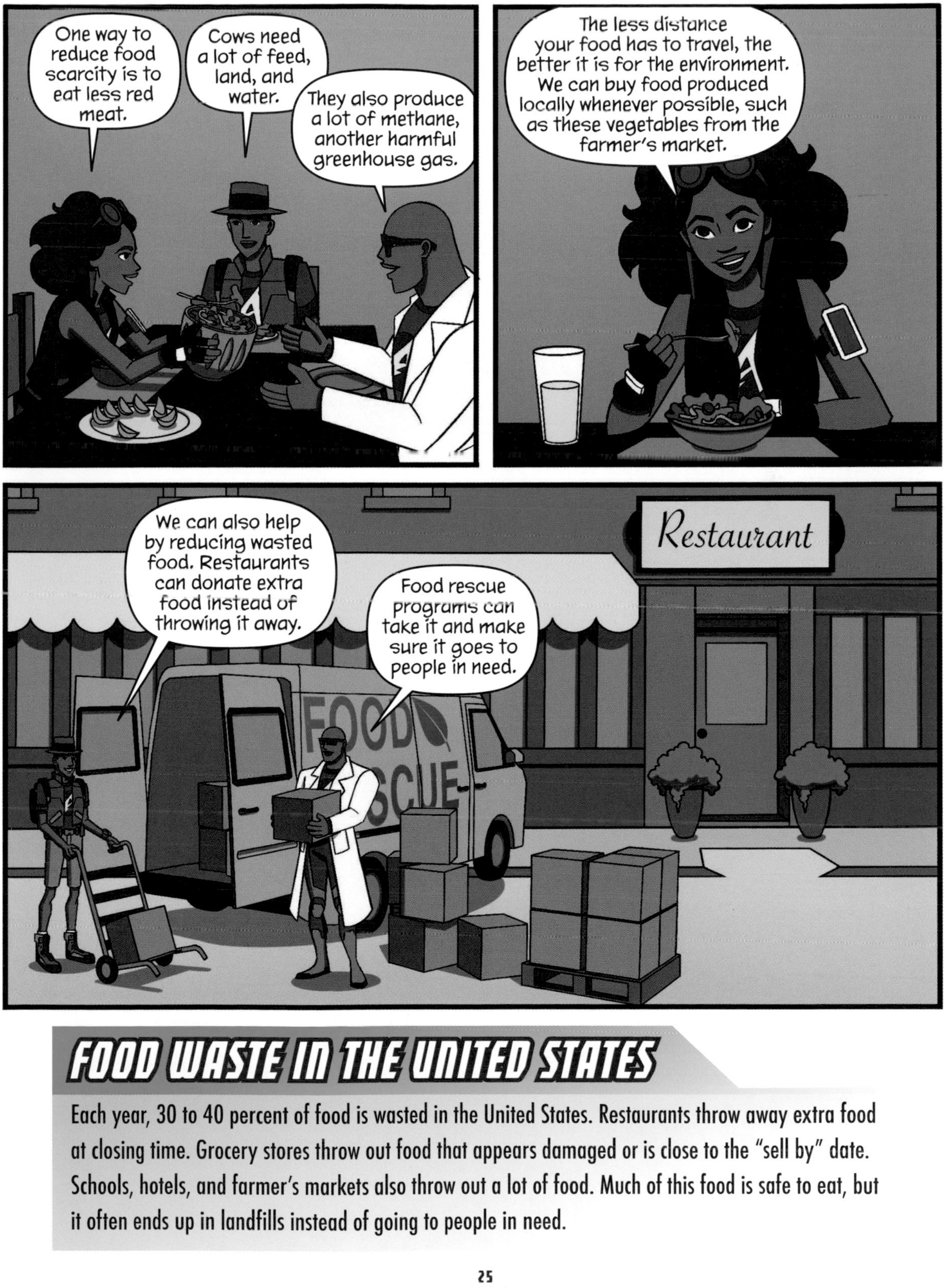
One way to reduce food scarcity is to eat less red meat.
Cows need a lot of feed, land, and water.
They also produce a lot of methane, another harmful greenhouse gas.
The less distance your food has to travel, the better it is for the environment. We can buy food produced locally whenever possible, such as these vegetables from the farmer's market.
Restaurant
We can also help by reducing wasted food. Restaurants can donate extra food instead of throwing it away.
Food rescue programs can take it and make sure it goes to people in need.

FOOD WASTE IN THE UNITED STATES

Each year, 30 to 40 percent of food is wasted in the United States. Restaurants throw away extra food at closing time. Grocery stores throw out food that appears damaged or is close to the "sell by" date. Schools, hotels, and farmer's markets also throw out a lot of food. Much of this food is safe to eat, but it often ends up in landfills instead of going to people in need.

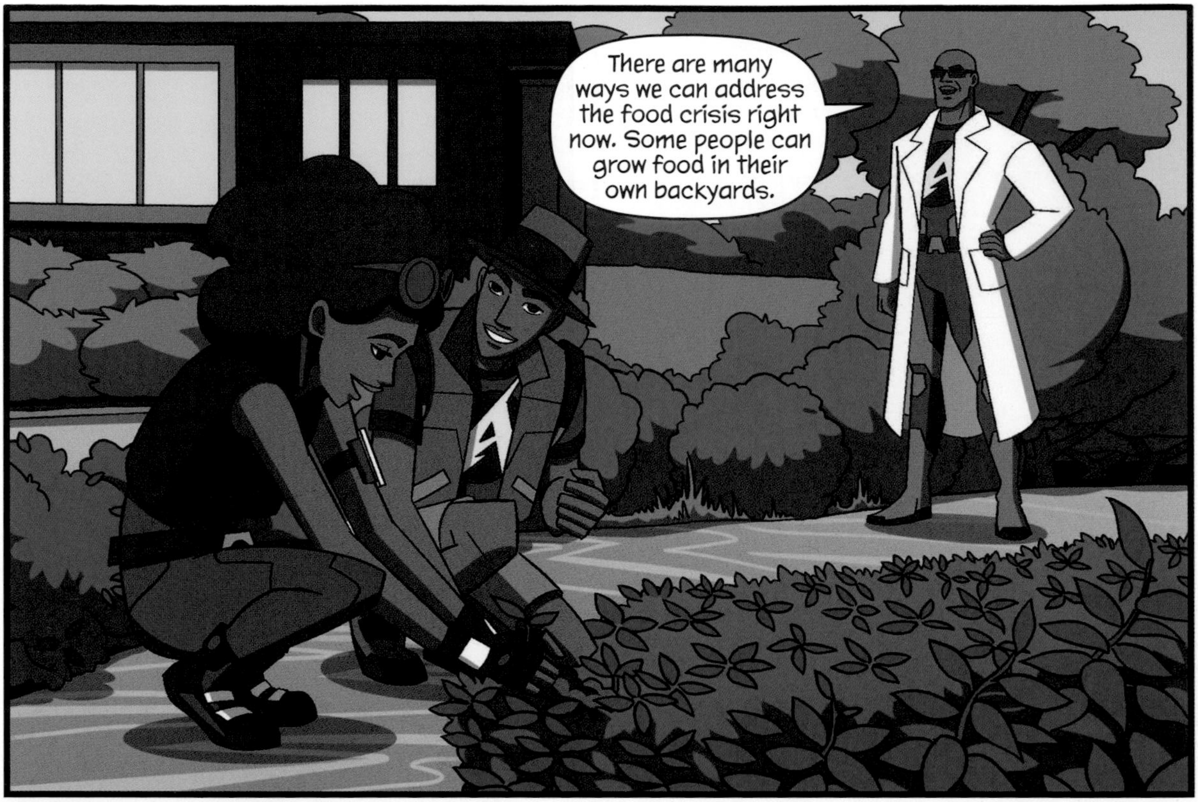
There are many ways we can address the food crisis right now. Some people can grow food in their own backyards.

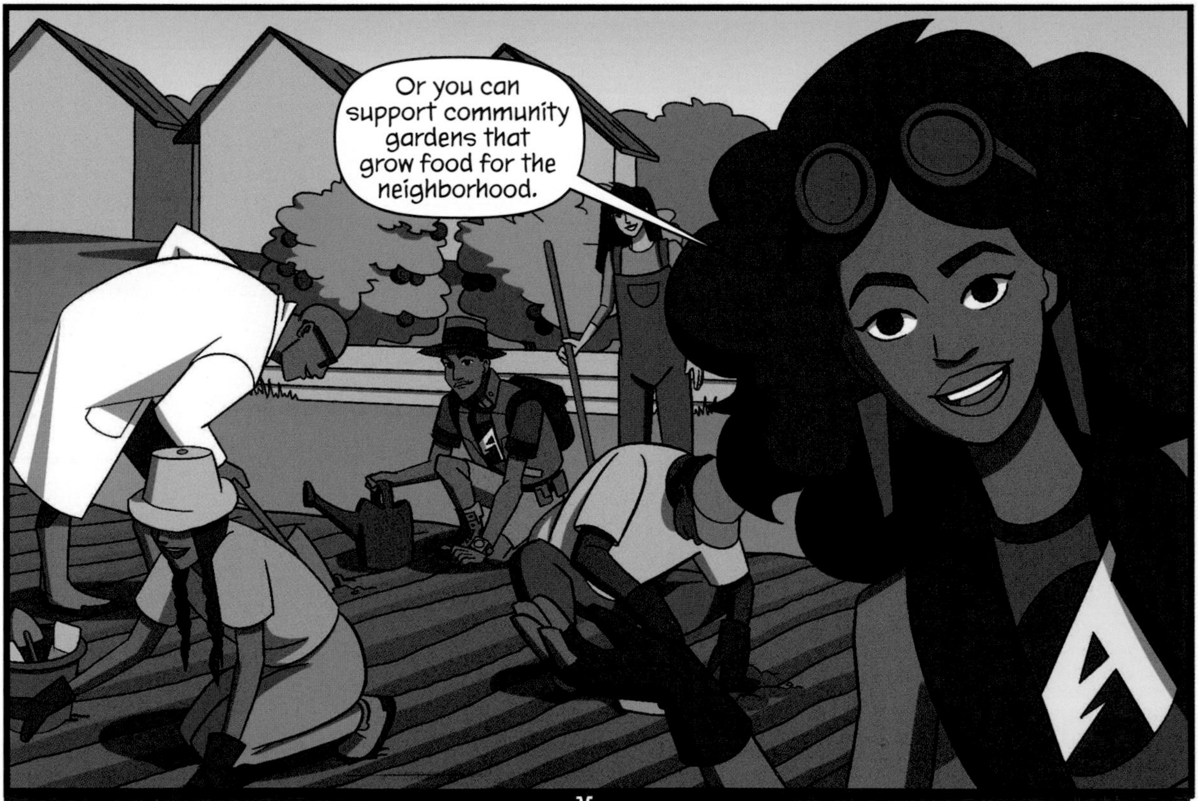
Or you can support community gardens that grow food for the neighborhood.

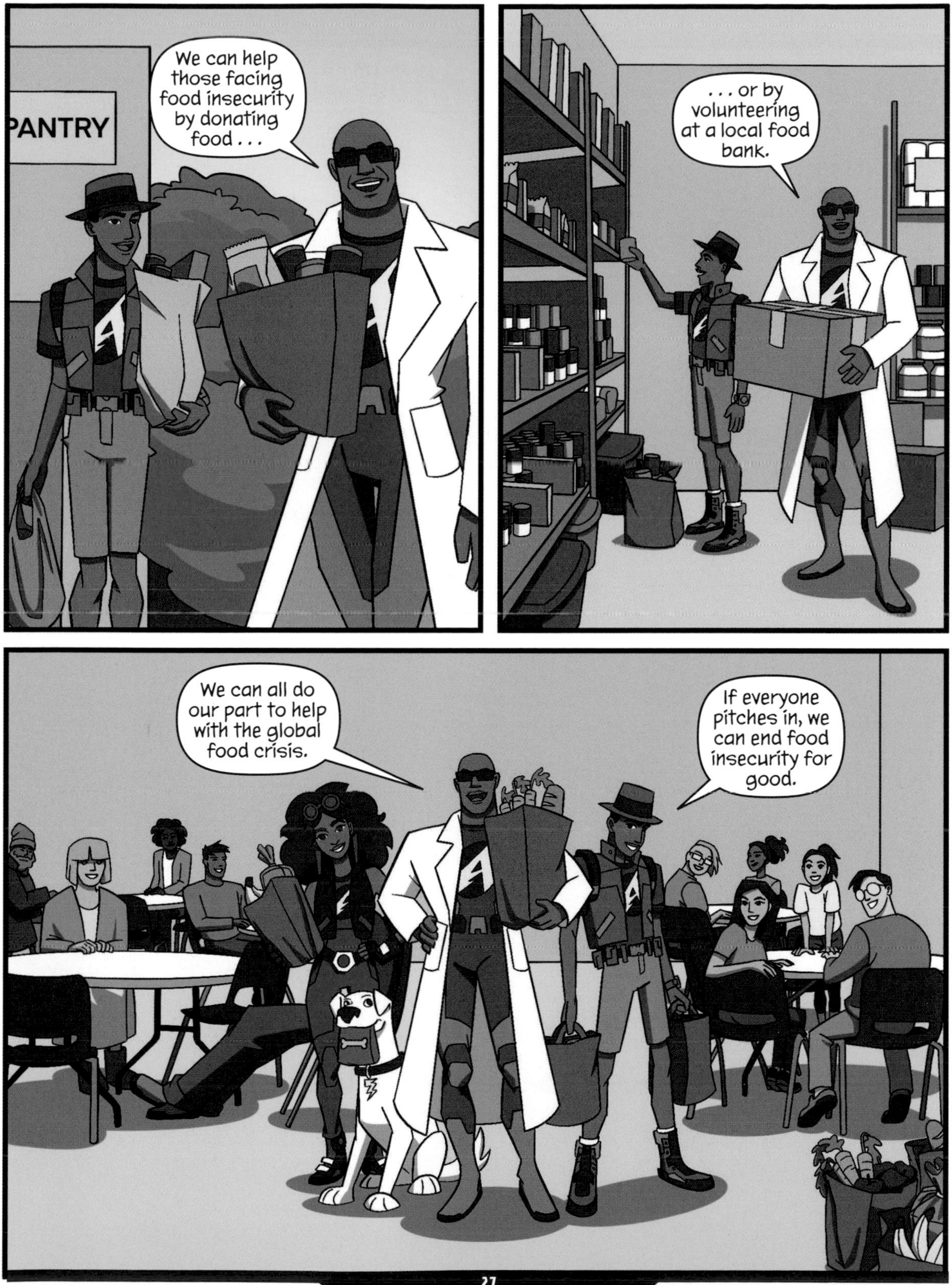
PANTRY
We can help those facing food insecurity by donating food . . .
. . . or by volunteering at a local food bank.
We can all do our part to help with the global food crisis.
If everyone pitches in, we can end food insecurity for good.

MORE ABOUT FOOD SCARCITY

Hunger and food insecurity don't mean the same thing. Hunger is the physical discomfort someone feels when their body needs food. Food insecurity means not having the resources to buy or obtain food.

Locust swarms often affect several countries at the same time. When this happens, it's known as a plague.

There are four types of droughts. When we hear the term drought, it often refers to a meteorological drought. This happens after long periods of dry weather in an area. Hydrological droughts happen when the supply from a natural water resource, like a river, runs low. If crops become affected it's known as an agricultural drought. Finally, socioeconomic drought happens when the demand for food exceeds the supply of available crops.

In the late 1960s, an Arizona businessman created the first food bank. John van Hengel got the idea while observing a mother looking for discarded food in a grocery store's trash bin. The woman mentioned that there should be a place like a regular bank that stored discarded food. Then people could "withdraw" the food when they were in need. Van Hengel soon established the first food bank. Others followed his lead. He eventually created Second Harvest, a network of food banks around the world.

Food Roof is an urban farm in downtown St. Louis, Missouri. It's built on top of a two-story storage facility. The organization grows more than 250 types of vegetables, fruits, and herbs.

Brooklyn Grange operates three separate rooftop farms in New York City. The farms grow more than 50 tons of vegetables each year!

GET INVOLVED

You and your family can help fight food insecurity in your community. Here are some ideas to get started:

- Try becoming a backyard farmer and grow crops for your family. If possible, plant extra crops that can be donated to a neighbor or at your local food bank.
- Start or maintain a community fridge or pantry. A community fridge is an actual refrigerator that is stocked with free food for anyone who needs it. These fridges are usually located outside a business that provides electricity. Others are located inside buildings like schools or community centers.
- Try to organize a food drive. Collect canned or dried food in your neighborhood that can be donated to a local food bank.

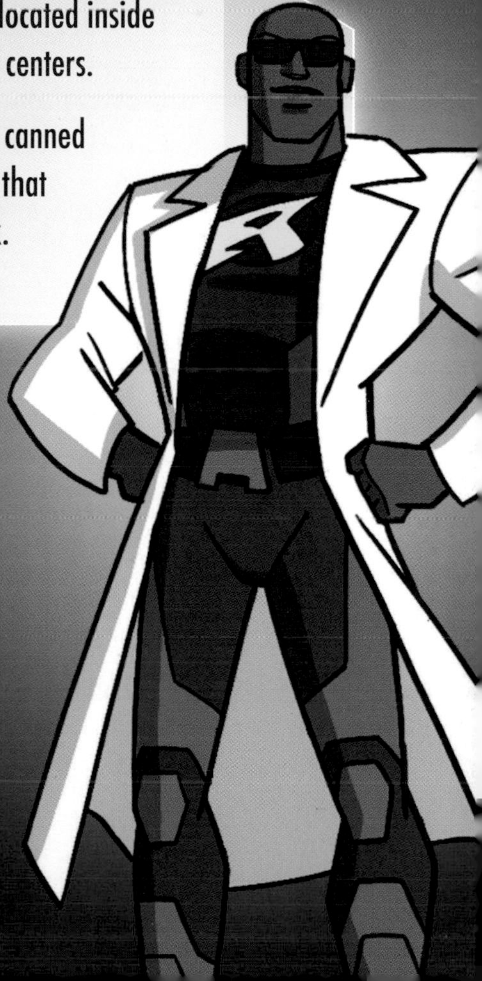

GLOSSARY

agriculture (AG-ri-kuhl-chuhr)—farming

environmental (en-VAHY-ruhn-men-tuhl)—relating to the natural world

evacuate (ih-VAK-yoo-ayt)—to leave a place for safety reasons

food insecurity (FOOD in-si-KYOO-rih-tee)—a condition in which people have limited access to food

hydroponics (hahy-druh-PON-iks)—the practice of growing plants in liquid nutrients rather than in soil

perishable (PER-ish-uh-buhl)—likely to spoil or go bad quickly

pesticide (PEST-uh-sahyd)—a chemical for killing harmful insects or other organisms

poverty (POV-uhr-tee)—having little or no money or means of support

recede (ri-SEED)—to go or move back

relocate (ree-LOH-kayt)—to move to a different location

scarcity (SKAIR-suh-tee)—a short supply of something

urban (UR-buhn)—relating to a city

READ MORE

Biskup, Agnieszka. *Understanding Global Warming with Max Axiom Super Scientist.* North Mankato, MN: Capstone Press, 2019.

Gilles, Renae. *Climate Change in Infographics.* Ann Arbor, MI: Cherry Lake Publishing, 2020.

Kurtz, Kevin. *The Future of Food.* Minneapolis: Lerner Publications, 2021.

INTERNET SITES

Easy Science for Kids
easyscienceforkids.com/food-insecurity

Junior Scholastic
junior.scholastic.com/issues/2019-20/120919/i-used-to-be-hungry.html#1120L

Wonderopolis
wonderopolis.org/wonder/why-is-world-hunger-still-a-problem

INDEX

ABOUT THE AUTHOR

Myra Faye Turner is a New Orleans-based poet and author. She has written for grownups, but prefers writing for young readers. She has written two dozen nonfiction books for children and young adults, covering diverse topics like politics, the Apollo moon landing, edible insects, and U.S. history. When she's not writing, she spends her days reading, napping, and drinking coffee.